The History and Hulley Families of the One House Rainow, near Macclesfield, Cheshire

Ray Hulley

Longview Publishing

February 2015

Published in Great Britain by Longview Publishing
Felden Lane Hemel Hempstead Herts HP3 0BB.
February 2015

ISBN 0-9540314-1-5 2nd revised and enlarged edition of ISBN 0-9540314-0-7 (1st edition)

All rights reserved. No part of this publication may be reproduced, stored in a retrieval system, or transmitted in any form or by any means, electronic, mechanical, photocopying, recording or otherwise, without the prior permission of the publisher.

Printed and bound in England by Parchment (Oxford) Limited, Cowley, Oxford.

Acknowledgements

I wish to thank the following organisations for allowing me access to various records that are quoted and/or reproduced in this booklet.

    The National Archives
    Cheshire Archives and Local Studies
    Manchester University John Rylands Library
    Manchester Central Library
    Macclesfield Express Newspapers

Grateful thanks are also due to Jasper Hulley of South Africa for permission to reproduce extracts from private papers and photographs of the Hulley collection, and to my sons Stephen and Alan for providing technical assistance in the preparation of this booklet.

Ray Hulley
February 2015

Contents

1.	The One House Story – before 1488	1
	Introduction	1
	Early One House references	1
	Development of the Hulley surname	3
	Locations of the Hulley surname before 1490	3
	The Hulley connection to the One House	4
2.	The Hulley family in the 16th century	6
3.	The Hulley family in the 17th century	9
4.	The Hulley family in the 18th century	13
	The church dispute	20
	Hulley's Volunteers	21
5.	The Hulley family in the 19th century	24
	The Hulley Coat of Arms	31
	A 19th Century Ghost	33
6.	The Hulley family in the 20th century	34
	An Abode of Gentry	37
	The demise of a 770 year-old house	42
	Appendix 1 Supporting Documents 1290 – 1348	48
	Appendix 2 Owners and/or tenants of the One House	54
	Appendix 3 Lease of the One House dated 1490	56
	Appendix 4 Deed by John Hulley of the nature of a Will c. 1500	57
	Appendix 5 Background Notes to the 1757 Church Dispute	58
	Appendix 6 Correspondence - Colours of "Hulley's Volunteers" 1912	60
	Appendix 7 General Report on the Hulley Pedigree	62
	Appendix 8 Petition for a Grant of Arms 1881	63
	Appendix 9 Hulley Coat of Arms - Details of Quarterings	65
	Appendix 10 The One House FamilyTree 1490 to 1927	67
	Index	68

List of Illustrations

Figure 1 The One House Rainow c1920s also known as Rainow Hall, Rainow Manor House	viii
Figure 2 Locations of surname variations 1302 to 1498	4
Figure 3 Obverse of One House lease dated 1490 (Cheshire Archives and Local Studies)	5
Figure 4 Reverse of One House lease dated 1490 (Cheshire Archives and Local Studies)	5
Figure 5 One House lease dated 1546	6
Figure 6 Decease of Laurence Howley 1567	7
Figure 7 Surrender of One House to John Howley 1567	7
Figure 8 Johes Howley shown in Jury List dated 1568	8
Figure 9 Lawrence Howley in Halmote Court List dated 1594	8
Figure 10 The marble font in St Michael's church, Macclesfield	15
Figure 11 18th century jug from the One House collection	17
Figure 12 Decorated jug with hunting scenes	17
Figure 13 Snuff box – gift to Jasper Hulley from his wife Ellen dated 1830	18
Figure 14 Silver beaker with One House monogram	18
Figure 15 Table cutlery with One House monogram	19
Figure 16 Soup tureen with One House monogram	19
Figure 17 One House grandfather clock c1770	19
Figure 18 Colours of the Loyal Macclesfield Volunteer Infantry	23
Figure 19 Uniforms of the Loyal Macclesfield Forresters and Volunteer Infantry in 1805	23
Figure 20 Surrender of the One House in 1806	24
Figure 21 1841 census of the One House	25
Figure 22 The One House shown on the 1850 Tithe map	26
Figure 23 1851 census of the One House	26
Figure 24 The Cottage, L'Hyvreuse, St Peter Port Guernsey birthplace of Sarah Ann Hulley	27
Figure 25 St George's, Castell, Guernsey. Residence of the Hulley family c1843-1855	27
Figure 26 1851 census of St George, Guernsey	28
Figure 27 1861 census of the One House	28
Figure 28 The late Jasper Hulley of the One House 1794-1867	29
Figure 29 1871 census of the One House	29

List of Illustrations – continued

Figure 30 The One House on the 1874 Ordnance Survey map	30
Figure 31 1881 census of the One House	30
Figure 32 Coat of Arms of Holland Hulley 1881	32
Figure 33 The 1891 census of the One House	33
Figure 34 The 1901 census of the One House	34
Figure 35 The One House shown on the 1910 Ordnance Survey map	34
Figure 36 The 1911 census of the One House	35
Figure 37 Sketch Plan of the One House in the Inland Revenue Assessment 1912	36
Figure 38 Front left corner of the One House with balcony	36
Figure 39 A view of the house from the walled garden across the back lane	37
Figure 40 A 1920s view of the One House. The tower is at the rear right hand side	38
Figure 41 View of carriage drive looking towards the front entrance on Buxton Road	39
Figure 42 View from north west corner looking towards the front right of the One House	39
Figure 43 The last Hulley family in the One House	40
Figure 44 The last known photograph of the One House c1930-35	41
Figures 45, 46 Demolition of the One House - exterior views	42
Figure 47 Front door with a stone lintel with inscription A.D. 1703 during demolition	43
Figure 48 Newspaper article - Ancient House Demolition	44
Figure 49 Newspaper advert - Stone Rubble	44
Figure 50 Hulley documents from South Africa prior to sorting and indexing	45
Figure 51 The front entrance to the One House on Buxton Road	46
Figure 52 The ornate front gate of the One House – now replaced.	46
Figure 53 The author's wife Joan at the One House rear gate	47
Figure 54 The view from the One House towards Macclesfield	47

Articles by the author

Date	Publication	Title of Article and/or Document transcribed
Aug 1990	NCFH	Hidden names in 17th century wills (A - G)
Nov 1990	NCFH	Hidden names in 17th century wills (G - Y)
May 1991	NCFH	The history and families of The One House (1)
Jul 1991	NCFH	The history and families of The One House (2)
Jun 1993	CA	Return of papists and dissenters in Cheshire Hundreds 1678-79
Mar 1993	M&L FHS	Unfilmed 1851 census of Manchester & district - progress report no. 1
Dec 1993	M&L FHS	Salford's Irish sardines
Nov 1993	NCFH	Macclesfield court rolls 1369-1370 (SC2 253/4)
Nov 1994	NCFH	Large goldmine found in Cheshire
Sep 1995	M&L FHS	Unfilmed 1851 census of Manchester & district - progress report no. 2
May 1996	NCFH	The bowling contest
Dec 1996	M&L FHS	Unfilmed 1851 census of Manchester & district - progress report no. 3
Dec 1996	M&L FHS	Irish immigrants in the unfilmed 1851 census for Manchester & district
Aug 1997	NCFH	List of deceased copyholders, 1706 (Bromley Davenport collection)
Dec 1997	M&L FHS	Unfilmed 1851 census of Manchester & district - progress report no. 4
Dec 1997	M&L FHS	1851 Prestwich migrants from Blackburn, Bolton, Bury and Wigan
Sep 1998	M&L FHS	Missing streets in 1851 census returns for Chorlton on Medlock
Dec 1998	PROFile	Transcription work on the 1851 unfilmed census Manchester and district
Dec 1998	CRO	Recognizances of Cheshire alesellers 1581 – 1634 (CHES 38/35)
Mar 1999	NCFH	Was your ancestor a 16th century Macclesfield seller?
May 2004	NCFH	The New Turnpike road between Macclesfield and Fernilee, Derbyshire
Mar 2000	M&L FHS	Unfilmed 1851 census of Manchester and district - progress report no. 5
Dec 2002	M&L FHS	Crickets Lane Fever Hospital Ashton under Lyne
Mar 2003	M&L FHS	Unfilmed 1851 census of Manchester & district - progress report no. 6
Jun 2004	M&L FHS	Unfilmed 1851 census of Manchester & district - progress report no. 7
Jan 2006	M&L FHS	Unfilmed 1851 census of Manchester & district - Final report no. 8
Nov 2007	NCFH	Rainow Assessments for Relief of the Poor 1750

Articles by the author - continued

Date	Publication	Title of Article and/or Document transcribed
Feb 2008	NCFH	Booth Family BMDs 1726
May 2008	NCFH	List of Voters in Rainow - Reform Act 1832
Aug 2009	NCFH	Knutsford Gaol List 1828
Nov 2009	NCFH	The Value of Different Estates in Ranowe 1696
Nov 2009	M&L FHS	My Own Olympic Hero!
Feb 2010	NCFH	Prisoners held at Chester Castle 1792 pt 1
May 2010	NCFH	Prisoners held at Chester Castle 1792 pt 2
May 2011	NCFH	1611 Survey of Macclesfield Manor and Forest
Nov 2011	MMU	Sporting Lives: John Hulley - Olympic Innovator
Nov 2011	Wikipedia	John Hulley 1832 - 1875
Spring 2012	Honey Pot	Liverpool's Olympic Innovator
Jul 2012	GOONS	John Hulley – British Olympic Instigator
Jul 2012	Oxford DNB	Hulley, John (1832–1875), promoter of physical education
Jan 2013	LHB	John Hulley and the Liverpool Heartbeat
Aug 2013	GOONS (Herts)	Robert C. Hulley – the Black sheep of one of my Family Trees
Nov 2013	NCFH	Macclesfield Court Rolls at The National Archives

Abbreviations

CA   Catholic Ancestor
CRO   Cheshire Record Office
DNB   Dictionary of National Biography
GOONS   Guild of One-Name Studies Journal
Honey Pot   Merseyside Pension Fund Journal
LHB   Liverpool Heartbeat charity - John Hulley magazine
M&L FHS   Manchester & Lancashire Family History Society – Manchester Genealogist
MMU   Manchester Metropolitan University Institute of Performance Research
NCFH   North Cheshire Family History Society – Family Historian
PROFile   Friends of the Public Record Office Magazine

Figure 1. The One House, Rainow c1920s, also known as Rainow Hall and Rainow Manor House

1. The One House Story – before 1488

Introduction

The One House was, by inference, the only house in the Forest of Macclesfield for many years. The precise starting point for it is lost in the mists of time but there remain several historical pointers as to an indication of its age. But before these are discussed, the history of Macclesfield Forest is a suitable starting point for this account.

Macclesfield Forest is an area of woodland, predominantly conifer plantation, located around 3 miles (5 km) southeast of Macclesfield in the civil parish of Macclesfield Forest and Wildboarclough, in Cheshire, England. The existing woodland is the last substantial remnant of the Royal Forest of Macclesfield, a once-extensive ancient hunting reserve.

The area is believed to have been occupied during the Bronze Age; there is a Bronze Age barrow near High Low Farm to the west of Macclesfield Forest and another earthwork east of the forest near Toot Hill. After the Norman Conquest the modern area known as Macclesfield Forest formed part of the much larger region of the Royal forest of Macclesfield, a hunting reserve owned by the Earls of Chester, which formerly stretched from the foothills of the Pennines east into the High Peak near Whaley Bridge and south to the Staffordshire Moorlands. The 'butts and boundes' were set down in the 1611 Survey of Macclesfield as "beginning at a Certain Bridge now called Awterspoole and so ascending the waters of Mercie *(Mersey)* to the water of Goyt and so ascending the water of Goyt to the water of Dane and so ascending the water of Dane to Crumwell *(Cromwell Wood)* and from Crumwell to the town of Rode then to the Town of Gawsworth along the way go the Town of Prestburie and from Prestburie to Norburie Lowe then to the Brook of Bosden to Saltersbridge then to the aforesaid bridge called Awterspoole". This was an area measuring approximately 16 miles north to south and 8 miles east to west – 128 square miles – 82,000 acres – considerably more than what the Forest is today!

The chief officers who had the custody of the Forest of Macclesfield on behalf of the King were a Master Forester and eight subordinate Foresters, whose office was hereditary. These officials were supported by the following persons, who undertook the duties shown:

a bailiff, who was responsible for collecting the rents of leases etc.;
a regarder, an overlooker of the Foresters and others who looked after the forests;
foresters, who looked after the game and watched for poachers;
a woodward, who combined the duties of forester and looking after the trees for which he was responsible.

Early One House references

The Master Forestership was conferred, about the year 1166, by Hugh Kyvelioc, Earl of Chester (1147-1181), upon Richard de Davenport, an ancestor of the Davenports of Davenport and Marton, and it remained in this family for many generations. The Lancashire and Cheshire Record Society's volume 126 page 180 reads as follows:

176. Charter making Richard Davenport master-forester of the forest of Leek and Macclesfield, and conferring on him 'Anhus' for his services as forester; in return for which grant Richard gave the earl a 'kazzorium sor bauzan' and two marks of silver and the earl's uncle, Richard, a 'kazzorium ferrant'.

Orig.: J.R.U.L.M. Bromley-Davenport Muniments, Deeds, Davenports of Davenport (i). Transcr.: B.L. Harl. MS. 2074, f. 78v., and Harl. 2038, f. 86 (new f. 92); Bodleian Library, Dodsworth MS. 31, f. 53v. Ed. Orm., iii. 61 (mutilated and inaccurate); *Stenton Misc.*, p. 38 (no. 10) (with facsimile): full English abstract, *Ches. Sheaf*, no. 9900.

This interesting charter marks the rise of the Davenport family. Its date lies between 1162, when Earl Hugh came of age, and 1175, the year of the death of his uncle, Richard, the son of Earl Robert of Gloucester and brother of Hugh's mother, Matilda. Roger Malfilastre also witnessed, c1165-1170, charters for Coventry Priory and for Humphrey de Bohun, and this probably gives the approximate limits of date. W.F. Irvine (Ches. Sheaf, no. 9900) identified Anhus with One House, 'an ancient stone mansion' in Rainow, 2 miles north-east of Macclesfield (Orm., iii. 771-2), and also suggested that 'kazzorium sor bauzan' is a sorrel skewbald hunter and 'kazzorium ferrant' an iron-grey hunter or possibly a blue roan.

This is the first documentation of the existence of the One House and several other references have been found between the above dates and 1490, when the house was leased by a Hulley.

There is a 111 year gap before the next reference to the One House is found. The Macclesfield Eyre Rolls of 1286 lists a Gilbert de Guhuz (taken to be Onhuz) as one of several persons who allowed their animals to wander in Macclesfield Forest. These entries are known as 'Escapes' and were essentially a licence to graze. The Eyre Rolls of 1290 lists 'Benedict and Roger de Onhus' giving 40d for release of the king's suit. There is clear documentary evidence to support the tenancies of the One House between 1290 and 1348 due to the existence of six Deed, Grant, Feoffment, and Quitclaim documents in the Davenport Deeds at Capesthorne. Full transcriptions of these documents are reproduced at Appendix 1.

In 1348 the house returned to the possession of the Davenport family by its granting by John de Passlegh and William de Weldon, Chaplains, to John de Davenport, Knight, and Margery his wife. This was the start of a 55 year period in which at least five generations of the Davenport family held the lease of the One House. Unfortunately although the names of each generation are known, the dates of their occupation are not. On the death of Edward Fitton in 1403, his widow Margaret settled her inheritance in Butley, together with the One House. After her death her eldest son Hugh inherited the estate. He died before 1443 and his widow Elizabeth Shaw eldest daughter of William and Joan Shaw, got tangled in a dispute with Thomas Duncalf the lawyer touching her rights of inheritance. The legal dispute between the two parties was settled in 1468, further details are shown in SC2 257/12 dated 1467-68 membrane 12. A list of owners or tenants of the One House is shown at Appendix 2.

In 1488-90 John Hulley was granted lease of 'a certain parcel of land containing one acre called Knolle House stydd with its appurtenances in the township (vill) of Rainow within the Forest of Macclesfield lately enclosed by the said John to him and his heirs forever, according to the custom of the said Forest, paying thence yearly to the Lord of Macclesfield for the time being one penny at the Feast of St Michael and also performing such other services as the other tenants of the said Forest are accustomed to do.'

The last sentence indicates that John Hulley had been granted tenancy of the Knolle House because of his occupation as an official of Macclesfield Forest. I later discovered from the 1611 Survey of the Manor and Forest of Macclesfield that Knolle House was a separate messuage of three roods within the One House estate, and was possibly the initial name of Grove Farm.

Development of the Hulley surname

It is generally accepted that the name is derived from a location or a series of locations, because there were several Hulley families in the north of England recorded as being from different counties either side of the Pennines.

I have searched through thousands of Macclesfield Court Rolls held at The National Archives in London and noted all Hulley and variant references from c1280 up to the 19th century. There are discernable patterns but it is almost impossible to assemble them in family groupings because of the paucity of detail in them.

The Macclesfield Eyre Rolls of 1275 -1296 contain many references to Hulle, de Hulle, del Hull, but the most consistent name that appears during this period is William de Holeye/Holey. He was a Regarder of Macclesfield Forest, whose responsibilities are recorded previously. This appointment was hereditary and descended from father to son and he was shown as such in 1285 and 1286. The de Holeye references in the Eyre rolls appear to be the derivation of later de Holey, de Hollay and de Hullay references in the SC2 rolls of 1350 - 1430. William de Holeye was listed in rolls up to 1307, and probably lived at Somerford because he acted as surety to Thomas de Somerford in a civil case concerning a tenement there in 1288. This village was also the home of John de Holeye, probably the son of William, who is recorded as being there in 1315 and 1322. John's wife Matilda also appeared in the court rolls of 1328 and 1329.

A 21 year gap with no Holeye entries ended in 1350 with the court appearance of Robus de Holey, who also appeared the following year as Roba del Holy and Roba Hulleson. Roba continued his court appearances in various guises including Roba del Hull, Roba del Hol, Robto de Holy until his last entry as Roba Holoy in 1361.

Meanwhile Adam had come on the scene in 1358-59 as Adam del Hull and Ad de Holey, He progressed through the court records in the 1360s as Ad de Hollay, Adam de Hollay, finally finishing the decade as – would you believe it – Adam Hulley! Admittedly he reverted to being called Holay and Hollay in 1372-1374, and Hulley/Hullay only appeared spasmodically between then and 1423 when there was a flurry of de Hulley and de Hullay entries until 1441. At this juncture the 'de' was dropped with Hulley and Hullay reappearing once more. 10 Hulley/Hullay entries are shown on court appearances between 1455 and 1467 (with Hauley used as an alternative to Hulley) and the 15th century ended with 16 court appearances by Hulley males, including John Hulley from the One House. From the above account, it will be seen how the surname developed over a 225 year period.

Locations of the Hulley surname before 1490

There are very few court roll entries showing a location for Holeye, de Holeye, Holey, Holy, Hullay and Hulley during this period. This was probably custom and practice as far as the court clerk was concerned. Macclesfield Forest covered an area of immense size in the 13th century, stretching from the River Dane in the south to the River Mersey in the north, from the river Goyt in the east to a line drawn from Offerton near Stockport to North Rode on the River Dane in the west. It included many townships and villages, some of which are listed in the above surname entries. Over a 200 year period pre 1500 these are as follows:

Date	Location	Date	Location	Date	Location
1302	Somerford	1406	Hyde	1469	Stalagh
1324	Somerford	1418	Bredbury	1485	Foxwist
1349	de Guyt	1424	Bredbury	1485	Mottram Andrew
1360	Hyde	1426	de Poynton	1489	Hale
1360	Newton	1432	Shrigley	1490	Butley
1367	Bosley Wood	1433	de Dokinfeld	1490	Rainow
1367	Mottram in L	1436	de Dokinfeld	1492	Adlington
1372	de Boslegh	1446	Dokinfeld	1495	Foxwist
1373	Mottram in L	1449	nup de Dokinfeld	1496	Ketulshulme
1381	Hyde	1456	nup de Hide	1498	Adlington
1400	de Norbury	1467	nup de Adlington		

Figure 2. Locations of surname variations 1302 to 1498

The spread of the surname raises some interesting possibilities. Those with locations in the north of the area including Bredbury, Newton, Hyde, Mottram in Longdendale and Dukinfield are considered a strong probability of being ancestors of the Hulley family of Dukinfield and Stalybridge, whose ancestry has been traced to circa 1555, but no written evidence exists to support this theory. The names shown in other locations i.e. around Macclesfield and the Forest are probably ancestors of the One House family which commences in 1490 with John Hulley, and are shown on the Cheshire-01 Family Tree.

The Hulley connection to the One House

The first, incontrovertible evidence of a Hulley family living at the One House is the 1490 lease – copied below and a full transcription is shown at Appendix 3 – between John Hulley and Ralph Davenport and his heir Hugh, descendants of the above family. A copy of this lease, together with many other family papers, is now held at Cheshire Archives and Local Studies at Chester under reference D 7392 Hulley family of Rainow records. The counterpart is held at the Manchester University John Rylands Library as part of the Bromley Davenport Muniments Reference Box 2/2 envelope 3/17/1-9 document ref 3/17/9.

Figure 3 Obverse of One House lease dated 1490 (Cheshire Archives and Local Studies)

Figure 4 Reverse of One House lease dated 1490 (Cheshire Archives and Local Studies)

2. The Hulley family in the 16th century

In c1500 John Hulley made a deed in the nature of a will in which he referred to the above lease.[1] A full transcription of his will is shown in Appendix 4. He assigned the One House to his wife Alice and his children Lawrence, Ellen, Margaret and Ann. His brother James, and Richard, William and Hugh, who were possibly other brothers, were also mentioned in the deed.

John Hulley died c1524 and his son and heir Lawrence was admitted to his father's lands in the Halmote Court of Macclesfield in September 1524.[2] By this time the annual rent had been reduced to a peppercorn of 1d per annum. Lawrence played a full part in the local community by being chosen as a juror of the Halmote Court no less than 102 times in the 41 years between 1526 and 1567. He was a party to a lease dated 30 September 1546 between Thomas Savage of Castleton in the County of Derby gentleman, Johem Showre Attorney and himself concerning the One House as shown below.[3]

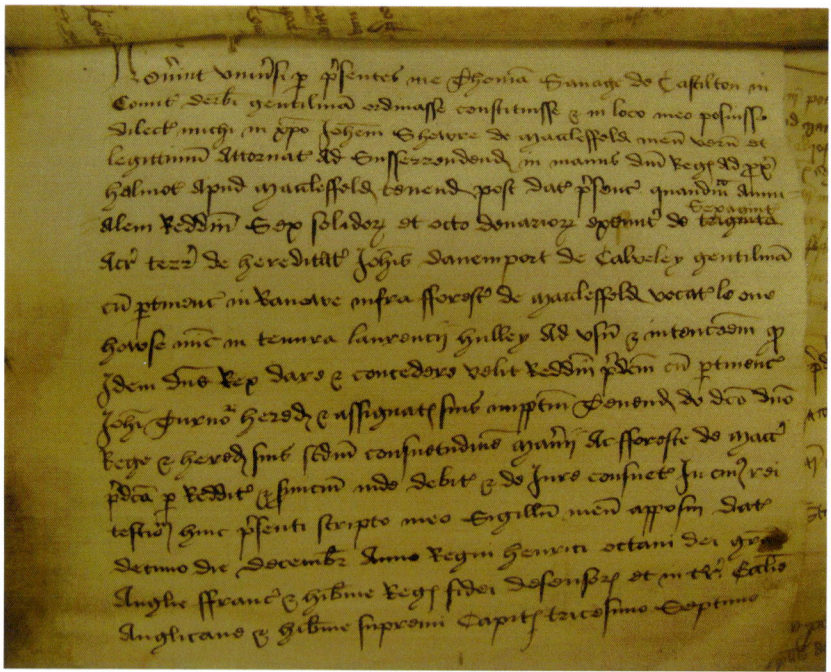

Figure 5 One House lease dated 1546

Laurence was appointed a constable of Rainow in 1548, together with Wyllyam Breson de Brynow but was on the wrong side of the law in 1551 when he was fined 2d for allowing 16 of his beasts to trespass in Macclesfield Forest. He was fined twice in 1556, this time for 6 beasts and paid a fine of 4d. His death in 1567 was confirmed by this entry in the Halmote and Great Leet of the Forest court roll.[4]

---
[1] Collection (Fonds) D7392 Hulley family of Rainow records Cheshire Record Office.(CRO).
[2] SC2 258/7 rev confirmed by LR 2/200 1611 Survey of Macclesfield page 207 at The National Archives
[3] SC 2/273/12 m 26 Hallmote and Great Leet of the Forest 1546 at The National Archives (TNA)
[4] SC 2/276/4 m 42 Hallmote and Great Leet of the Forest 1567 at TNA

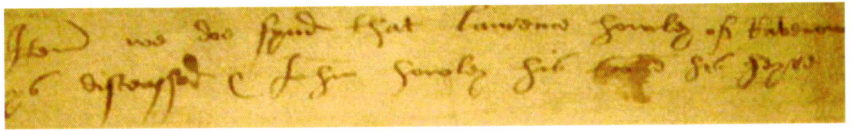

Figure 6 Decease of Laurence Howley 1567

Transcription:- Item we doe fynd that Lawrence Howley of Ravenowe ys disceassed & John Howley his sone his heyre.

The following extract from the Halmote Court rolls dated 1567 at The National Archives (TNA) shows the surrender of the One House to John Hulley. The first line reads "Johes Howley de Ranow in Com Cestre filius et heres Laurent Howley in ppr psona venit hre in plen Halmot "[5]

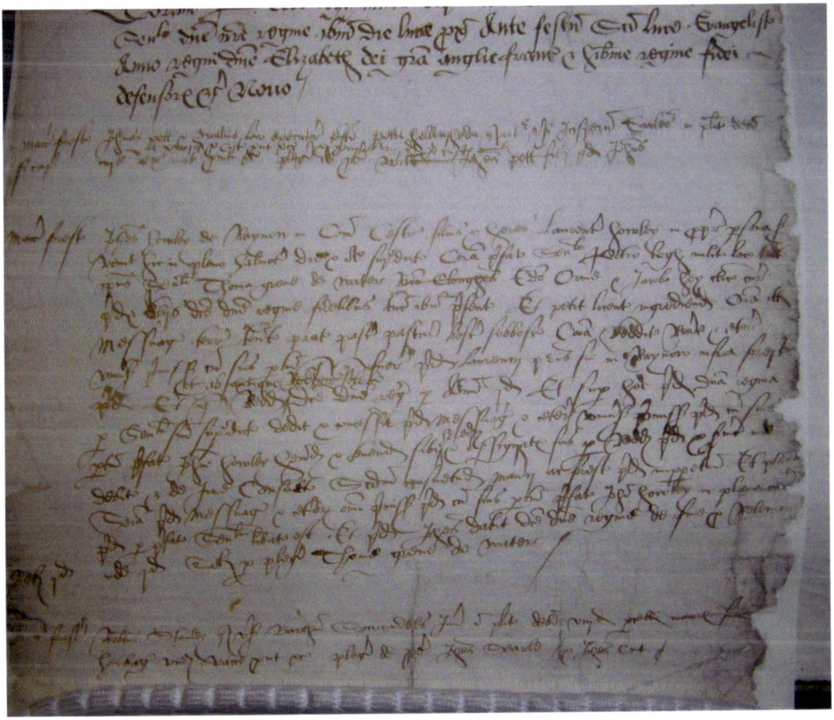

Figure 7 Surrender of One House to John Howley 1567

No baptism entry exists for John Hooley/Howley but his marriage to Ellen Fowden on 14 October 1561 was recorded in the registers of St Peter's church Prestbury. They had 2 children – Lawrence and Henry. No baptism records exist for either child but both must have been born before 1572, the year of their mother's death.

---

[5] SC 2/276/4 m 39 Hallmote and Great Leet of the Forest 1567 at TNA

Like his father, he was appointed a juror and the rolls show that he was called for jury service on 32 occasions, mainly in the Swainmote Court. The entry below is for jury service in 1568.[6]

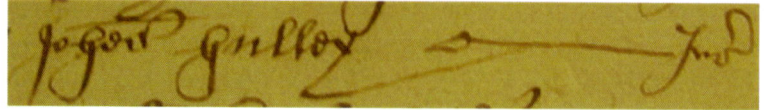

Figure 8 Johes Howley shown in Jury List dated 1568

One of John's last duties before his death was to agree a quitclaim with Thomas Turner. I was unable to find an entry in any court roll but the following transcription is from the Hulley Family Papers from South Africa reference 6 transcribed by the Cheshire historian John Earwaker.

To all persons &c. **Thomas Turner** of Bollington co. Chester, yeoman, sends greeting. Know ye that I the said **Thomas** in consideration of a certain sum of money to me paid by **John Hooley** of Ranow co Chester yeoman, have released and forever quitclaimed for me, and my heirs to the said **John Hooley** all my right, title &c. to certain lands in Ranowe aforesaid and also have quitclaimed to the said **John Hooley** a certain rent of 6s. 8d arising from certain premises in Ranowe aforesaid, and late in the occupation of the said **John Hooley** or of **Hugh Davenport** of Calveley co. Chester Esq., to the only use of the said **John**, his heirs, and assigns for ever. With the usual clauses of warranty.
Dated 30th August 29 **Elizabeth** 1587. Seal gone.

John died and was buried at St Michael's church on 9 Feb 1587-88. Lawrence became heir to the One House estate on the death of his father in 1587 and his brother Henry went on to marry Elizabeth Burgess and form the Howley family of Macclesfield Park, a dynasty lasting over 120 years. The One House family under Lawrence expanded in the closing years of the 16th century with his marriage to Kathleen Jackson in February 1588-89, and the births of John in 1590 and Thomas in 1595. Lawrence was empanelled as a juror in the Portmote and Swainmote courts on 12 occasions up to 1600. The surname had changed several times during this century, and at least 12 variants have been recorded from different sources. Hooley was first used in 1563 and Howley in 1581.

In 1594 Laurance Howley was shown in a list of names – "Those fyned for not appearance at the great Leet houlden in the xxxvj yeare of her Matesh raigne". For some reason he wasn't fined for his non-appearance.[7] He is shown on the last line of the document below.

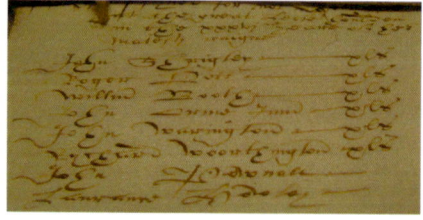

Figure 9 Lawrence Howley in Halmote Court List dated 1594

---
[6] SC 2/276/6 m 11 Hallmote and Great Leet of the Forest 1568 at TNA
[7] SC 2/280/6 m 10 Hallmote and Great Leet of the Forest 1594 at TNA

3. The Hulley family in the 17th century

Lawrence Howley and Kathleen continued to have children in the early years of the 17th century, and Ellen (1600), Alicia (1612) and Thomas (1615) were born at the One House. This place was listed in the 1611 Survey of the Manor and Forest of Macclesfield, and it is worth repeating the actual entry in full.

Customary Tenauntes (Rainow):- p307

LAURANCE HOOLEY claymeth to hold to him and his heyres according to the custome of the said Manor and forrest, as heyre to **JOHN** his father, by copie of Comptrol dated 4 die Decembris Ao. Dno. Eliz. XXXJ. *[1589/1590]*[8] in Ranow aforesaid, vidzt,

One Dwelling house of three bayes, One kitchen of one baye, One barne of 4 bayes, and one out Ho., and two bayes at the end for beaste and ewes. Three other bayes for haye and beaste, One kilne of a baye, one garden, and one fold, One messuage called the knowle, by est 3 roods. Yearely Valew 1li. Yearely Rent 4d.

Memorandum that the Jurors aforesaid psent and saye, that **JOHN HOOLEY** his father hath the same house and no more and his grandfather **LAWRENCE HOOLEY** lykewyse, paynge herefore but the yerelie rent of -----1d. And upon the Copie of the admittance of the said **LAWRENCE** the grandfather Ao. XVJ RR H: 8. *[1525/1526]*[9]

And also upon the Copie of the admittance of the said **JOHN** Ao. IX. Rne **ELiz:** *[1567/1568]* the yearlie rent expressed to be due for the pri....es was 1d. And it is alleged by the said **LAWRENCE HOOLEY** that he never useth to pay therefore any more than the yerely rent of one pence, albeit that the rent of iiijd be expressed upon the aforesaid Copie dated iiijto die Decembris Ao. Rne Eliz. XXXI. *[1589/1590]*.[10]

In 1616 Lawrence Howley and his wife Kathleen appeared at the Consistory Court at Chester as witnesses in a case concerning their daughter Ellen and her relationship and ultimate marriage to Thomas Oldfield. The result of the case is not known but the Notes of Lawrence contain interesting material relative to the case.[11]

Lawrence's eldest son John married Katherine Willott of Tiderington (sic) in 1621. They had three sons – John died 1622, Jasper born 1625 and another John born 1630. This was the first generation with a Jasper, named after the father of Katherine Willott. Jasper as a first name was to re-occur at regular intervals throughout future generations and even today there are three living males with this name.[12]

In 1622 Lawrence's father-in-law Jasper Willott and three others granted John senior one close of land in Rainow called Le Harre Esburie at an annual rent of 7d.[13] Although he owned land in Rainow, John preferred to live at Tidderington, his wife's home village in the early years of his marriage.

In 1623 Lawrence Hulley signed a new lease for the One House with Arthur Davenport of Calveley which included the latter's right to mine and carry away coal from the One House lands. The rent rose to 21s 8d per annum plus two 'rent capons' at Easter. As part of the new lease Lawrence also had to 'finde, provide for, have in readines, and sell forth, one

---

[8] SC 2 276/4 folio 39 dated 26 Dec 1567 at TNA
[9] SC 2/272/6 m3 Hallmote and Great Leet of the Forest 1523-24 at TNA
[10] LR 2/200 page 307 Survey of Macclesfield Manor and Forest 1611 at TNA
[11] Consistory Court of Chester EDC 5/34 Prestbury 10 Oct 1616 at Cheshire Record Office
[12] See South Africa 02 Family Tree.
[13] Copy held in the Collection (Fonds) D7392 Hulley family of Rainow records at CRO.

sufficient and Able Billman, with a plate coate and a sculle, to serve and attend upon the said Arthur Davenporte and his heirs in the warrs aforesaid.[14] John's wife Katherine was now added to the One House lease in 1625 as part of her marriage settlement and the estate expanded to include two closes called the Walles, part of the Lower field, the Barrfield and the Toote-hill field.

The One House estate expanded again in 1626 with the lease of 40 acres of common or waste land in Rainow at an annual rent of 10s 6d. This transaction is shown on a document[15] held at The National Archives and includes a reference to Lawrence and John, sons of Lawrence (senior) and Katherine the wife of John. Another 8 acres of common land was added to the One House lands in 1630 at an annual rent of 2s.[16] This land was almost immediately split into three lots, one of which was assigned to John Hulley and the remainder left with his father Lawrence.[17]

John's land holdings increased in 1630 with the lease of 5 acres of land called Edesburie Grounds at the annual rent of 15d.[18] This land was later held in trust to secure payment of £30 advanced to a Davenport in Nantwich.[19] After his first wife Katherine died in 1631, John senior again leased more land, this time one acre in Rainow on the east side of Macclesfield Forest called Girdshawe Brooke.[20] John married Elizabeth Greene on 26 September 1635 at Prestbury Parish Church.

"Lawrentius Hooley de One-house infra Ranowe" died in 1639 and the estate passed to his eldest son John who had been living at Tidderington up to at least 1635. On the 28 April 1651 John Hooley attended the Halmote court to surrender "All that his Messuage and tenement situate lying and being in Ranowe." This was re-granted by the court to Thomas Jackson of Ingarsley, John Lowe of S...., James Oldfield of Sutton and John Johnson of Hanforth. It is not known why this action was undertaken, because in September 1653 the above-named Thomas Jackson brought a Warrant of Attorney to the same court under the hands and seals of William Griffith of Carnarvonshire and Elizabeth his wife proclaiming that the 42 acres of land in Ranowe currently occupied by John Howley should be surrendered and re-granted to the said John. This was agreed to by the court and John paid a fine of 15s for the privilege.[21]

In 1663 the One House estate was surrendered by John Hulley and re-granted to William Clowes of Langley and others 'for the purposes contained in an indenture dated 29th July 1662.[22] No record of this indenture has come to light at the present time so it is assumed that the One House was temporarily granted to the other party in the indenture. It was shown on the Hearth Tax returns of 1663 (Rainow – John Howley ij chargeable)[23] and on a copy dated 1675 of a return of 1663 (Ranow – John Houley 4 hearths).[24]

John Howley made a will[25] in February 1674-75 and died one year later at the One House. His will shows him as 'John Howley thelder of the One House' with his wife Elizabeth as a beneficiary. Also named were his five children living at the time of his death – Jasper b. 1625; John b.1638 married Judith Brontnall 1663; Edward b.1640 married Elizabeth Oakes

---

[14] ibid
[15] ibid
[16] ibid
[17] ibid
[18] ibid
[19] ibid
[20] ibid
[21] ibid
[22] ibid
[23] E179 86/145 at TNA
[24] E179 244/34 at TNA
[25] Original held at CRO –copy held

1674; Thomas b.1642 married Sarah Oakes 1672; and Charles b.1642 married Hester Oldham and who died in 1689. It specifically mentioned two closes of land in Rainow – 11 acres lying upon Keridge and three and a quarter acres upon Billinge. The former was left to his son Edward and the latter to his son Charles.

John Hulley's will gives a good insight of his worldly goods and possessions, including items in the One House. These include inter alia 'the new press in the parlor, her (i.e. his wife's) trunke, a great brass Candlesticke, a pewter dish which was her mother's, a paire of new iron bound wheels, a cart chest, an axletree, kipes boards, axletree pines, washers, the jacke in the kitchen, two bedsteds, a table, and a forme, another table and a forme, one dishboard, one chest and the Clock in the house.' He was a generous person and left money to the local poor i.e. 20s to the Macclesfield poor, 13s 4d to the Rainow poor and 6s 8d to the Hurdsfield poor. He also left money to his children and grandchildren as follows:

John Howley (son)	£16
Edward Howley (son)	£10
Charles Howley (son)	£70
John Howley (grandson)	10s
John Jackson (godson)	12d
John Hulme	12d
Francis Watson	12d

He left 'my great bible' to Jonathan Howley, his grandchild. This is probably the same bible that Holland Hulley loaned to John Earwaker to extract the family's birth, marriage and death entries over 200 years later in 1881.

The surprise in John Hulley's will was that he left nothing except a bedstead to his eldest son Jasper. Indeed, he was quite vitriolic in his reference to him. 'And I doe hereby declare of a truth that my said son Jasper hath noe right to any of my goods within my dwelling house or elsewhere, but only one seeled bedsted, and hee hath another of myne. Let him have whether of them he will.' Whether this is the outcome of a family feud we may never know, and although no mention is made of the inheritance of the One House by Jasper, the 1684 will of his brother Edward Howley of The Hough Wilmslow identifies 'my brother Jasper of the One House in Ranowe.[26]

Jasper Howley the new incumbent in the One House had married Rebeccah Booth in 1661-62 and had had the following children by the time he inherited the estate from his father: Jonathan b.1662; Josiah b.?; Jasper junior b.1667; Joseph b.1669; Anthony b.?; Samuell b.1673; Abigail b.?; and James b.1679.

Jasper's eldest son Jonathan married Dorothy Holme, daughter of James Holme, at Gawsworth in Aug 1690. The marriage settlement was written in an Agreement[27] dated 7 July and included the payments of £270 by James Holme and £60 by Jonathan Howley, both to Jasper Howley. In addition, the One House and other properties were to be held in trust for the life of Jonathan and Dorothy.

Locations mentioned in this agreement include the following:

The One House	Jasper Howley
Newly erected dwelling	William Boothby *(continued over)*

---
[26] ibid
[27] Copy held in the Collection (Fonds) D7392 Hulley family of Rainow records at CRO.

Goodshaw	Edward Walker
Messuage in Macclesfield	formerly Peter Deane now Jasper Howley (son)
the Frostcroft	the Ridge meadow the Barrfield
the Barrfield meadow	the Great Edsbury
the Cliff road	the further Knowl
the Spring march	the Moore[28]

Several of the above were re-granted to Jonathan by a Deed dated 20 August 1691. These were the Higher House Barn, the Great Haybay, the further Knowl, the Spring marshe, the Little Cliffe, the Great Edsbury and 24 acres of the Great Moore.

The One House Deeds dated 1691 (the onehouse within Ranowe) lists Jasper Howley as head together with Rebecca his wife, Jonathan his eldest surviving son and heir, and Josiah Howly his second son Josiah married before 1700 and moved to Blackley, north of Manchester where he and his unknown wife had two children, Booth b.1770 and Rebecca b.1701, each named after their grandmother Rebeccah Booth. Because of the later occurrence of Josiah as a first name in the Hulley family of Hurdsfield, (Josiah b.1744 and Josiah b.1791), Josiah may have returned to Cheshire and started this line. This must remain speculation until confirmatory evidence is available.

---

[28] ibid

4. The Hulley family in the 18th century

Jasper Hooley died intestate in 1700 and administration of his estate was granted to his widow Rebecca. The One House passed to his son Jonathan who was evidently keen to follow in his father's expansionist footsteps and after having the One House newly fronted in 1703 (the initials I.D.H. - Jonathan and Dorothy Hooley - were placed over the door), purchased the Bottfield and Watson's meadows in 'Edesbury' from William Watson of Swanscoe. However these lands and the Roefield, Sprinck, and Rushey meadows were granted to Thomas Braddock and Joseph Lowe in 1729.[29]

Jonathan was appointed constable of Rainow in 1714 and 1715[30] and purchased land etc in Rainow from Joseph Lowe called the Marple. He was described as "Jonathan Hulley of Walln House in Rainow Gentleman".[31] He purchased further land when Edward Tompson of Keyridgend in Ranow surrendered land in Ranow called Keyridge to him in 1725.[32]

In 1729 both Jonathan and his eldest son Jasper were involved in a case in Chancery against the Right Hon. The Lady Bridget Viscountess Dowager Fauconberg. Jasper Hulley was the plaintiff in the case and claimed recompense for services alleged to have been rendered by him to the defendant. Many interesting facts about Jasper and Jonathan his father are shown in the case papers. Jonathan was 66 years old at the time and was employed by Lady Fauconberg as a Commissioner. A deponent claimed that he 'had frequently observed him to sit at Table at Dinner and Supper with her and never heard her blame or commend the Complainant.'

In his deposition Jonathan said that in 1717 he put his son Jasper as Clerk or Apprentice to William Latus of Manchester, Attorney at Law to learn and be instructed in the profession of Law. He gave Mr Latus £64 10s for a bound apprenticeship commencing 1 January 1717 for four years. His son completed the apprenticeship successfully and remained with Mr Latus for another six months. He then went on to say that Lady Fauconberg wanted his son 'to come with all Expedition to her at Sutton Hall and that there were letters from London which must be answered.' He eventually received a letter from the defendant wherein she expressed herself well pleased with the conduct and management of his son in her affairs and that if his knowledge and parts were well known 'there would not be so many knaves and fools employed' or words to that effect.

The Exchequer class at the PRO has several papers relating to the case[33], which was heard in the Baron's Court of his Majesty's Court of Exchequer at Westminster. These include lists of Interrogatories to the deponents of both complainant and defendant. Jasper Hulley's deponents had up to 19 questions to answer, whilst those of Bridget Fauconberg had to reply to up to 17 questions. Jasper Hulley had the following persons to depose in his favour:

> Ann Jenkins of Oxford Street, London, wife of Edward Jenkins, coachman, who had known Jasper for three years and Bridget for six years. She was the latter's servant at Sutton Hall in 1726, with her husband probably employed as her coachman. (Date of deposition 4 July 1729).

---

[29] Copy held in the Collection (Fonds) D7392 Hulley family of Rainow records at CRO.
[30] SC 2/319/1 Court Leet of the Manor and Forest - Forest Constables 1714-15 at TNA
[31] SC 2/346/4 m3 Proclamations for Surrenders 1724-25 at TNA
[32] SC 2/346/5 m1 rev Proclamations for Surrenders 1725-26 at TNA
[33] E 133/70/47 and E 134 3 Geo 2 Trin 3 at TNA

William Booth of St Mary's Islington, gentleman. In 1726 he acted as go-between to Jasper and Bridget when she wanted him to act as her Steward to collect rents etc. for an annual salary of £100 plus 'horsehire and expenses.' He would be in place of 'Mr Lunt her late Steward who had defrauded her of large sums of money.' (Date of deposition 4 July 1729).

John Pearson servant to the Rt. Hon. Lord Orrey. He was previously butler to Bridget Fauconberg. (Date of deposition 14 October 1729).

Bridget Fauconberg called Eliza Lawley to speak for her. She had known Jasper for two years and Bridget for three years. Three years prior to the case, she had witnessed at the lodgings of Lady Bridget in New Bond Street 'Lady Fauconberg deliver to ….. Jasper Hully a large sume of money consisting of some hundred pounds but how many she this depont. cannot set forth.'

The case was first listed in July 1729[34] and it was ordered in Michaelmas term 1729 that it be heard in the next Hillary term.[35] On 27 January 1729-30 Mr. Kettleby the counsel for Lady Fauconberg sought the referral to the Deputy of the King's Remembrancer to tax her former solicitor Mr Barber's Bill of Fees and that the Office Copy of the Answer of Jasper Hulley be deducted from him and left with the Deputy.[36] These requests were agreed to and Mr Barber was ordered by the Court to deliver up his bill of Fees and disbursements, which were then ordered to be taxed and settled by Lady Fauconberg. He was further ordered to deliver up all papers and writings relating to the case and deposit the Office Copy with the Deputy to the Court.

I spent considerable time trying to establish the outcome of the above case. The Exchequer Entry Books, which show case results, were searched for the period 1728 to 1731[37] without success, as was the Entry Books of Orders on the King's Remembrancer side of the Exchequer for the period 1729 to 1755.[38] From analysis of the entries in the Order Books it appears that Lady Fauconberg sacked her counsel and engaged a new one. This may well have resulted in the case being settled out of court in 1729.

The relationship between Jasper Hulley of the One House and Lady Fauconberg appeared to be very strong before he brought the above case. She made a formal agreement with him on 18 February 1726-27 for him to be her Steward and Receiver of Rents from her properties in Cheshire and Nottinghamshire. There is evidence of Jasper travelling to London on several occasions with Lady Fauconberg and Ann Jenkins tells of when, in December 1726, Jasper and Lady Fauconberg travelled to London together. He was absent from Chester for 13 weeks and her deposition continues: 'During a fortnight or more of that time the Complt. was closely confined with the Deft. the Lady Fauconberg at the Katherine Wheel Inn in Bishopsgate Street, and that during the rest of the time or most part of it the said Complt. was constantly with the said Deft. at her lodgings where he was employed by her from morning till evening in her Chamber in writing several things according to her direction.' In a letter dated 31 July 1727 from her to 'Mr Jispar Hulley at the Bell in Bell Yard near Temple Bar' Lady Fauconberg discusses payment by Jasper to various persons. She ends her letter with the words 'pray return with all speed to Sutton (i.e. Sutton Hall) I was never so maloncoly in my life, & as much alone as in ye deserts of Arabia, I need say no more.' Other deponents mention Jasper staying at Sutton Hall with Lady Fauconberg.

---

[34] E 127/35 1729 Trin no. 165 ibid
[35] E 127/35 1729 Mich nos. 170 & 246 ibid
[36] E 127/35 1729 Hill no. 185 ibid
[37] E 126/24 and /25 ibid
[38] E 127 ibid

The Rainow branch of the Hulley family was now well established in local circles and another branch – that of Macclesfield Town – was about to match them. This branch had been formed by the marriage of Jasper Hulley b.1667, third son of Jasper of the One House and younger brother of Jonathan, to Hannah Heywood. The newly married couple made their home in Macclesfield and over the next 23 years had 12 children: Mary b.1691; Alice; Hannah b.1693; Elizabeth b.1695; Jasper b.1697; Rebeccah b.1701; Thomas b.1703; John b.1705; William b.1708; Jonathan b.1709; Josuah b.1712; and Sara b.1714. Two of their children married their One House cousins – Mary (b.1691) married Jasper in 1730 following the trauma of his court case against Lady Fauconberg and just before he inherited the One House on the death of his father Jonathan; and Elizabeth (b.1695) married John Hooley of Macclesfield (Jasper Hulley's younger brother and formerly of the One House) in 1734.

The Macclesfield branch of the One House dynasty became an integral part of the Macclesfield scene during the early part of the 18th century with father Jasper and younger sons Thomas and John all occupying the mayoralty of Macclesfield at various times. Jasper was elected mayor in 1709-10, following his election to alderman in the previous year. Thomas was mayor in 1744 but unfortunately died whilst in office. He left in his Will[39] 'ten pounds to be laid out in the purchase of a Marble Font of Derbyshire Marble for the use of the Parochial Chappel of Macclesfield.' The marble was quarried in the immediate area of Moneyash and is still in the parish church. It is the only font that I have seen with wheels! It must have travelled many miles during its existence, because it is easily and frequently moved around the church for the convenience of christenings. The inscription, now missing but originally attached to the font, read: "The gift of Thomas Hooley obiit xvi Sep. MDCCXLIV in his mayoralty." John preceded him in 1741-42 and served a second term in 1748-49.

Figure 10 The marble font in St Michael's church, Macclesfield

---

[39] Original held at CRO –copy held

The death of Jonathan Hooley of the One House in 1730 and the succession of his eldest living son Jasper was formally confirmed by an entry in the Court Leet of the Manor and Forest on 15 Oct 1730 which stated "We do find Jasper Hulley of Rainow gentleman to be eldest son of Jonathan Hulley gentl. deced. to be ye next heire at Law to all such Copyhold Messuages, tenements, landes and hereditaments as ye said Jonathan Hulley ye father was seized or ntituled to be at ye time of his death lying & being in Rainow or elsewhere within ye said Manor & forest of Macclesfield."[40]

When Jonathan Hulley died in 1730 he left his second wife Alice and 8 children – Jasper b1696, to whom he left the estate, Hannah (who had married Thomas Clark), John, Elizabeth, Amye (who had married John Bresne), James, Jonathan and Elizabeth (who had married Francis Worthington).

The Chancery case between Jasper Hulley and the Right Hon. The Lady Bridget Viscountess Dowager Fauconberg in 1729 has been covered previously on pages 13 and 14, because it occurred during the life of his father Jonathan, who was a witness in the case. After the death of his father, Jasper was married at St Michael's church Macclesfield to his cousin Maria Hulley of Macclesfield, sister of Thomas Hooley who was the mayor of Macclesfield in 1743, by Licence.[41] Jasper was admitted as an Attorney on 17 Nov 1730 by Mr Justice Price at Serjeant's Inn, London.[42] He followed up this award by being admitted a Burgess of Macclesfield on 9 August 1832.[43]

In 1731 Jasper bought the Har Edsbury parcel of land and in 1732 he was sworn in as a Burgess of the Borough of Macclesfield. Jasper's second marriage was in 1750 to Elizabeth Forster and in 1759 he married Mary Lowndes. He had three sons – Jonathan b1703, Samuel b1737 and Thomas b1740, and two daughters Maria b1731 and Susanna b1742. He was elected a Governor of Macclesfield Free Grammar School in 1750 and in 1757 he gave permission by means of an Indenture[44] for copper ore to be extracted from the One House land by Bryan Hodgson of Buxton, and Charles Roe and John Stafford both of Macclesfield. In 1759 he decided to surrender certain parts of the One House estate. These included dwelling houses in Edsbury Lane, Hurdsfield and Rainow, the Rainow Poor House, (between Tower Hill and the River Dean, below the War Memorial) and the Roefield and Rushey meadows (on Buxton Road above Eddisbury Hall carriage drive) also in Rainow.

Jasper died in 1772 and left the One House to his eldest son Jonathan, who had previously married Mary, the daughter of one of his neighbours, John Arderne of the 'Oaks' at Sutton. Like the Hulleys, they were also landowners and had the distinction of having a branch of the family in Warwickshire, from which William Shakespeare's mother was derived. Jonathan and Mary had nine children: Jasper b.1755; John b.1757; Martha b.1758; John b.1759; Mary b.1760; Hannah b.1761; Jonathan b.1762; Thomas b.1764; and James b.1767.

In the 18th century it would have been quite natural for residents of the King's hunting Forest of Macclesfield to enjoy the field sports of the period and the Hulley family of the One House would have been no exception. The following images demonstrate the typical pastimes of the landed gentry reproduced on pottery from the One House collection. The

---

[40] C 2/319/66 Court Leet of the Manor and Forest 15 Oct 1730 at TNA
[41] St Michael's church Macclesfield registers 24 Sep 1730.
[42] Lists of Attorneys and Solicitors - 1729 - 1730 Page 66 at TNA.
[43] Collection (Fonds) D7392 1732 Hulley family of Rainow records at CRO
[44] Copy held in the Collection (Fonds) D7392 Hulley family of Rainow records at CRO.

jugs are the property of Mr. Jasper M. Hulley of South Africa and are reproduced with his permission.

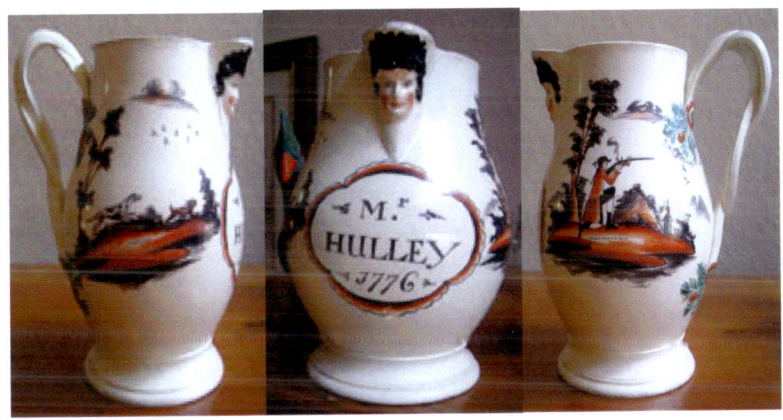

Figure 11 18th century jug from the One House collection

Figure 12 Decorated jug with hunting scenes

Figure 13 Snuff box – gift to Jasper Hulley from his wife Ellen dated 1830

Figure 14 Silver beaker with One House monogram

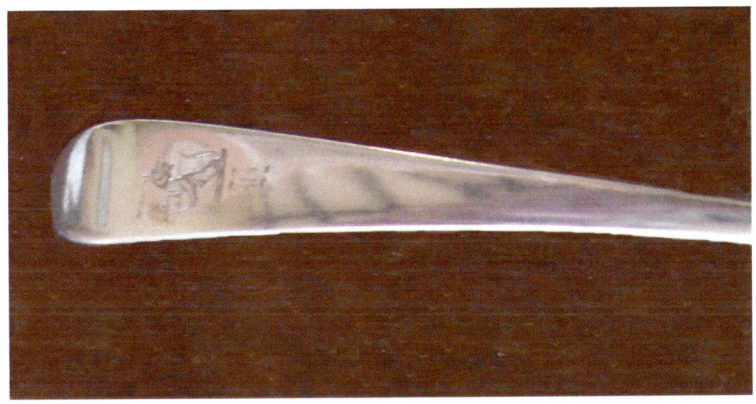

Figure 15 Table cutlery with One House monogram

Figure 16 Soup tureen with One House monogram

In 1779 the One House estate consisted of the following (tenant's names in brackets):

The One House	(Jonathan Hulley)
Messuage on One House land	(John Rhodes farmer)
Messuage on One House land	(Robt. Boothby, Benjn. Bennett farmers) (formerly Thos. Hulley, Peter Boothby)
The Goodshaw messuage & land	(John Wilkinson - formerly tenanted by) (Joseph Warren)
Har Edsbury land	(John Jackson - formerly Jasper Hulley)
Windyway Head messuage	(James Taylor)
The Brink land	(Jonathan Hulley and William Swindells) formerly Thos Rowson & Samuel Norbury
Grove Farm	(Tenant unknown - purchased in 1779)
Knollnoak	(John Rhodes - tenant farmer)

Figure 17
One House grand
father clock c1770

19

Jonathan died in 1786, leaving almost £2,000 (£226,000 at today's purchasing value) between his remaining children Jasper, Jonathan (who at the time of his father's death was a potter living in Stoke on Trent), Thomas, Martha and Mary. Jasper Hulley b1755 inherited the One House and purchased two parcels of land in Macclesfield Park called the Sharpley or Lower Fields and one parcel of half an acre previously owned by Henry Higginbottom. Ten years after his father's death Jasper further expanded the estate in 1796 by purchasing land adjacent to Swine Park, formerly part of Macclesfield Common. He was the last member of the family to be honoured as mayor in 1794. The family had now established itself as one of the important dynasties in the area at this time and appeared to be in an unassailable position. However, this was destined not to continue, as the events of the early 19th century were to prove.

Before we leave the 18th century there were two events which occurred in Macclesfield and district that had quite an effect on the towns- and village-folk. In each instance, the Hulley connection was an important part of both events.

The church dispute

Dispute in 1755-57 concerning the liability of the inhabitants of Rainow and other Outlying Townships to contribute towards the expense of keeping Macclesfield Church in repair

This matter had been a festering sore between the inhabitants of Macclesfield and those of the surrounding villages for over a century and was caused by the church insisting on the outlying villagers paying for the upkeep of the church. Appendix 5 outlines the main points of the case; this was written by John Earwaker in c.1850 and is useful background material.

In 1737 the inhabitants of Macclesfield applied for a Writ and afterwards took down a side of the chapel and built one without consulting or advising with the various townships to the charge of which they contributed. The new chapel, although much enlarged, was still too small even for the inhabitants of the township of Macclesfield itself. Nor were there any seats or room for any of the inhabitants of the outlying townships to sit in except a very few which some of the inhabitants had purchased. For these reasons several of the said townships had built chapels of their own for divine worship, and kept and maintained preaching ministers at their own expense. Many of them had also refused to pay the annual fees to Macclesfield church.

A High Court suit was instigated against the villagers, presumably by the Consistory Court at Chester in 1754, ordering the villagers to pay as requested. This was ignored and in 1754 a libel suit was raised against three specimen defendants of 3 of the villages involved. These were as follows:

Rainow - Jasper Hulley; Pott Shrigley - John Downes; Wildboreclough - Robert Pott.

Libel papers were served against Jasper Hulley in 1756 but the result of the case is not known. A number of documents covering many aspects of this matter are held in the Collection (Fonds) D7392 1732 Hulley family of Rainow records at CRO under the reference C. Church Dispute 1755-57.

Jasper Hulley died in 1772 and although the dispute was settled in favour of the Townships, the possibility of an Act of Parliament making the townships pay after all had been raised. In 1774 Jonathan Hulley of the One House wrote the following letter to a Mr Alford at Lyme Hall, who presumably was the private secretary to Mr Peter Legh.

Sir

I shall take it as a Particular favour if you will represent to your Mr. the Hardships ye Sevral Townships have suffered under ye Parochial Chapel of Maxfd. in making them subject to a Law Suit for many years past and notwithstanding ye suit carried on in ye spiritual Court was given in favour of ye Townships; proposals are now made to obtain an Act of Parliament to cause ye Townships to pay according to Assessmt. by yt to be granted.

My late Father has declared that when anything Extraordinary has been done at ye Chapel which has occasioned a greater Ley, the Townships by desire have made a Subscription to assist in paying that Ley: but afterwards an assessmt was made on ye Townships to compell, it was refused, which causd ye Litigation; and therefore as I understand Mr. Legh has connections with us in having a property in Kettleshulme, and perhaps in other of ye Townships, I beg that he will take it into Consideration and at this Juncture to stand our friend (as we are subject to ye Leys of the Parish Church and have Chapels of our own to take care of).

Please to make my Complts to Mr. Legh with respect to yourself who am
                    Your Hnble Servt.   J. Hulley
One House   30 Nov 1774

Whether Peter Legh responded positively or not is not known; a search of the Acts of Parliament passed between 1774 and 1780 failed to find any Act associated with the subject in question.

Hulley's Volunteers

In response to an appeal from the Government of the day, who were concerned about the possible invasion by French troops, Jasper Hulley of the One House formed the Loyal Macclesfield Volunteer Infantry. His request to assist the country in the military action was first highlighted in a report in the London Chronicle dated 18 Mar 1797.

Commissions in the Supplementary Militia, for the County Palatine of Lancaster, signed by the Lord Lieutenant; dated Jan, 16, 1797. To be Lieutenants (Incl), Jasper Hulley.

Also in the Dublin Gazette of 27 June 1797.
    Macclesfield Volunteer Infantry. Jasper Hulley, Esq.; to be Captain.

Further documentary evidence to support his intentions is a report in "Historical Records of the 6th Administrative Battalion Cheshire Rifle Volunteers" dated c1920.

> The same month, *[August 1797]* a Company was formed at Macclesfield under Captain Jasper Hulley; A second Company was added to the Macclesfield Corps, and Captain Hulley, the only one of the old Officers remaining, now received the title of Captain Commandant. This Officer took the greatest interest in his Corps, equipping the men at his own expense, and was afterwards offered a Majority, *(ie promotion to another Regiment)* which, however, he declined. He died in 1807, and was succeeded by Captain James Pearson. The Colours of this Corps hung for some years in the parish church, but being Taken down when the church was re-painted, were considered by an enlightened official too shabby to be re-placed; they are now carefully preserved in Captain

Hulley's family. The Queen's colour is of dark blue silk, with the Royal Arms in the centre. The Regimental colour is of crimson silk, with the Union in the upper canton; in the centre, within a wreath of oak leaves and acorns, are the arms of Macclesfield - a lion rampant, holding a garbe, or; and underneath, the motto, "Nec Virtus nec Copia desunt."

A letter from J[oseph (sic)] Hulley, Captain, Macclesfield Volunteer Infantry, to Lord Stamford[45] reads:

> J. H. has sent regular returns of the Macclesfield Volunteer Infantry to the Adjutant General and Henry Dundas. Asks Lord Stamford to obtain Government gunpowder and flints for exercises.

Known colloquially as Hulley's Volunteers, the Corps consisted of the following ranks and men:

2 Captains	4 Lieutenants	2 Gunners
1 Quartermaster	1 Surgeon	1 Sergeant Major
8 Sergeants	8 Corporals	9 Drummers/trumpeters
160 Privates		

A return of the numbers of men in the Corps on 3rd May 1804 showed the following:

No. of Companies	- 2
Subalterns	- 8
Date of Services	- 1803 Aug. 20
Establishment	- 100
Sergeants	- 8
Total	- 200
Corporals	- 8
Field Officers	- ---
Drummers	- 4
Captains	- 2
Rank and File	- 200
Allowances	- Pay ---
Clothing	-- 20/- per man

The Corps headquarters was at Warrington but they did most of their drilling and practicing in the Old Church Yard in Macclesfield. When the regiment was disbanded in 1805 their colours were deposited in the church and later given to the Hulley family for safekeeping. Correspondence during 1803, 1804 and 1805 between Captain Hulley and Prince William Frederick and Earl of Stamford and Warrington, Lord Lieutenant of Cheshire is held at The National Archives and copies are shown in the Notes for Jasper Hulley 1755-1806 in years 1803 and 1804.

---

[45] ELGAR system Ref: GB 133 EGR4/1/2/16/50 dated 2 Oct 1798 Scope and Content- held at the John Rylands University Library Manchester.

Figure 18 Colours of the Loyal Macclesfield Volunteer Infantry

Jasper Hulley provided all uniforms for the 200 men plus officers at considerable expense to himself.

LOYAL MACCLESFIELD FORRESTERS AND VOLUNTEER INFANTRY, 1805.

Figure 19 Uniforms of the Loyal Macclesfield Forresters and Volunteer Infantry in 1805

The fate of the Colours 110 years after they had been raised was the subject of correspondence in the Macclesfield Courier and Herald in October 1912. This is reproduced in Appendix 6.

5. The Hulley family in the 19th century

Jasper Hulley of the One House died in 1806 and Jasper junior b1795 inherited the estate. He was the third son of his generation to be christened Jasper, the other two having died in 1793 and 1794 respectively. The surrender and transfer of the One House was recorded in the Halmote Court rolls dated 24 March 1806.[46]

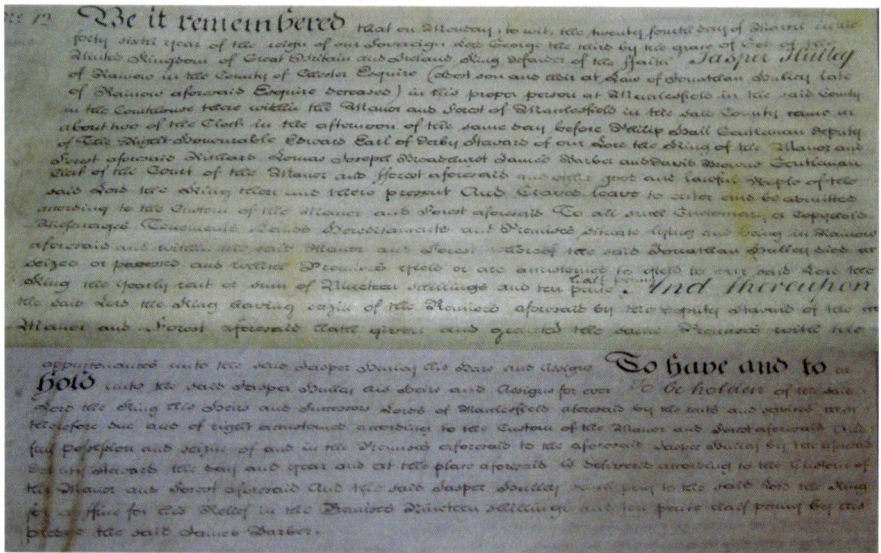

Figure 20 Surrender of the One House in 1806

Jasper was clearly too young at 11 to be able to pick up the reigns of the estate at his father's death and his mother decided to sell the One House estate. It was advertised in 1815 with the following details:

Farm/land/messuage	Occupier
The One House	Mary Hulley widow
Shady Yard Green (Sutton)	Robert Greaves
Grove Farm	Joseph Sheldon and Martha Sutton
Windyway Head Public House	Geo. Preston .
Eddesbury Lane Farm	Alexander Hooley/Hulley (son of Jasper of Hurdsfield b.1756)
Three fields called Eddesburys	Widow of Peter Arnold
Bott Field Farm	Martha Hammersley
Marsh Rails with five fields	John Rhodes
Two Ridge Meadows & Barfield Leys	Thomas Barnes
Vale Royal	Thomas Hesford (formerly Jeffery Mottershead)
Walker Barn messuage/public house	William Heald

Later in the same year certain parts of the estate were again offered for sale, but for some unknown reason the One House was not sold at this point, in spite of the efforts of Mary

---
[46] SC 2/307/3 f9 ref 12 Halmote of the Manor and Forest 24 Mar 1806 at TNA

Hulley. This may have been fortuitous, because her son Jasper Hulley of the One House is recorded as being elected to the post of High Constable of Macclesfield Hundred in 1829. He married Ellen Bostock who bore him Jasper b1824, Mary b1826, Ellen Elizabeth b1828 and Harriet b1831. Ellen died in 1832 and Jasper remarried Maria, daughter of Philip Holland of Hordern in 1833. Their first boy was called Holland Hulley after his second wife's maiden name. Coincidentally a son in the Holland family was called Jasper Loton Holland, after Jasper Hulley. His next two sons were also named after families – Gorton and Arderne. Four girls completed his family, making 11 children born between 1824 and 1844.

The 1841 census[47] shows Jasper and Maria, together with 5 of their children at the One House. They also had 4 servants, thus demonstrating the continued wealth of the family.

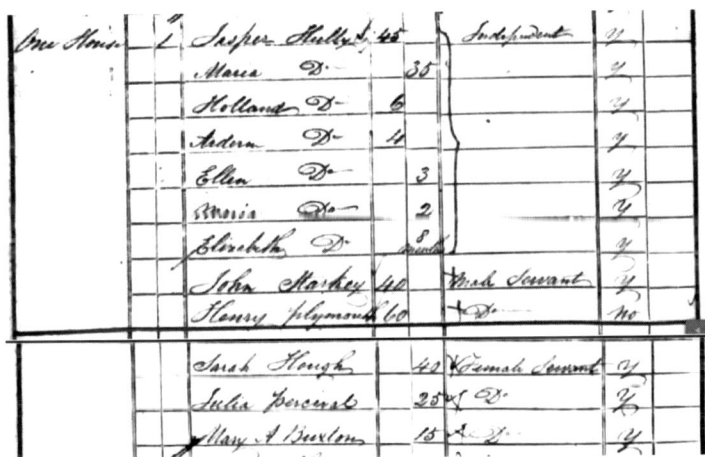

Figure 21 1841 census of the One House

The next event affecting the Hulleys of the One House was many miles away from Cheshire – in Guernsey, Channel Islands, in fact! This was the birth of Jasper's youngest daughter Sarah Ann who was born at Hyvreuse, St Peter Port, Guernsey on 10 July 1844.

The columns of the Macclesfield Courier from 7 June 1841 – the day after the 1841 census – and the Jasper Hulley entry in the Cheshire Electoral Registers dated 1842 were searched for clues as to when the family left Rainow to live in the Channel Islands. The following entry dated 2 October 1841 was found suggesting that Jasper Hulley was still living at the One House on that date:

Game Lists – County of Chester; First Publication. Persons who have obtained Game Certificates for the year 1841: List 1 – General Certificate at £4. 0s. 10d. Incl. Hulley Jasper, Rainow.

This implies that the family left the One House between 2 Oct 1841 and early 1842. Other evidence to support this was that the abode of Jasper Hulley on the 1842 and 1843 Electoral Registers was shown as St Peter Port, Guernsey.

---

[47] HO 107/106 Book 12 folio 14 at TNA

On 20 November 1842 the furniture in the One House was offered for sale in the Macclesfield Courier. This action was probably taken after the family had left Rainow and were leasing the property.

The following six lots of the estate (with tenant's names) were again advertised for sale by auction in the Macclesfield Times in 1846:

The One House	Matthew Gibbon	60 acres
Grove Farm	John Kirk	83 acres
Knoll Nook	Alice Rhodes	23 acres
Eddisbury Lane Farm	Mrs. Sheldon	16 acres
Bottfield House Farm	James Broadhead	16 acres
Windyway Head Farm	Joseph Bennett	56 acres

The sale notice went on to say: 'The Mansion House forms a spacious residence for a Gentleman's family. It commands an extensive and beautiful view of the lower part of Cheshire, and is well sheltered with full grown Timber and younger Plantations, in which there is a fine Rookery. The Outbuildings and Offices are extensive and substantially built. The Farm Houses and Outbuildings are of stone material and slated, well timbered, and sufficiently commodious. The Lands are principally cultivated as Meadow and Pasture, yielding an herbage of excellent quality. The Estates abound in Coal mines, which are now in the course of being worked.'

Figure 22 The One House shown on the 1850 Tithe map

814 Plantation
815 One House Mansion (2 buildings)
815a House, Outhouse and Garden
1816 Knoll Plantation

Not shown on map:

806 Rookery
807 One House Meadow
808 Palfrey Meadow
809 Plantation
810 Little Pasture Meadow
811 Kitchen Garden and Croft
812 Plantation

The 1851 census[48] covering the One House lists James and Matthew Gibbon in residence and there is a gap of ten years before the Hulley family reappears.

Figure 23 1851 census of the One House

[48] HO 107/2159 folio 60 at TNA

The family were still living in Guernsey in 1851 but had moved to a place in western Guernsey called St George. This was a 'large and lovely estate' with attractive grounds in the middle of which was a grey stone building behind which was one considerably older. The census entry[49] shows Jasper Hulley Landed Proprietor, Maria his wife and seven children, all of whom except Mary, the eldest were classed as scholars being taught at home. A cook, housemaid and dairymaid supported the family. The reason for the family's move to Guernsey is not known; poor health and/or the need of a better climate may have been factors but no firm evidence has to come to light to date.

In 1994 during a holiday in Jersey, I travelled to Guernsey to establish where the family had lived in the 1840s. Aided by the birth certificate of Sarah Ann dated July 1844 and the 1851 census entry, I traced them to Hyvreuse, St Peter Port and St George.

Figure 24 The Cottage, L'Hyvreuse, St Peter Port, birthplace of Sarah Ann Hulley

Figure 25 St George's, Castell, Guernsey. Residence of the Hulley family c1843-1855

---
[49] HO 107/2531 folio 288 and reverse at TNA

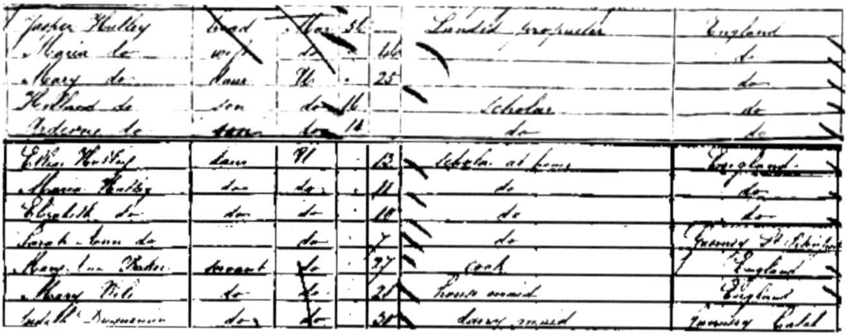

Figure 26 1851 census of St George, Guernsey [50]

The above census shows that Maria, Elizabeth and Sarah Ann were all being taught at home by a private tutor, and the family had a cook, housemaid and dairy maid to look after them.

The One House census return of 1861[51] shows Jasper and Maria plus three daughters and a stepdaughter. Either because of the lower number of family members or because of financial problems, the servants had now been reduced to three.

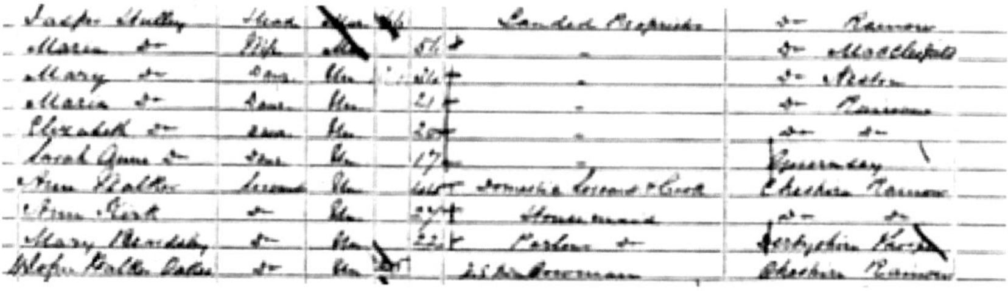

Figure 27 1861 census of the One House

Sometime between 1841 and 1861, Arderne Hulley had left the One House, joined the Navy and settled in South Africa, where he married Fanny Cecelia, the daughter of Arthur Clarence, the High Sheriff of Natal. He had married into the South African gentry and his two sons, described as 'Gentlemen', were destined to join them. Descendants of this branch are shown on the South Africa-02 family tree on the website at www.hulley.info. Holland Hulley disappeared from the family scene for several years, but a letter written in 1925 from Philip Holland to Done Hulley (1877-1935) in Natal, South Africa disclosed that Holland had spent some years in South Africa prior to 1865, when he bought land and kept sheep and cattle; a record of baptisms in South Africa show that Holland was a godfather in 1870 and 1877, before returning to England in time for the 1881 census.

Jasper Hulley died suddenly at the One House of a heart complaint on the 11th August 1867 at about four o'clock in the afternoon, aged 72 years and nearly 11 months, leaving the One House estate in trust to Maria his widow, Loton Holland his neighbour and brother-in-law of his sister Mary, and Holland Hulley, his eldest son, who had the option to purchase the estate – at a valuation – within three years of his father's death.

---
[50] HO 107/2531 folio 288 and reverse at TNA
[51] RG 9/2577 folio 42 at TNA

Figure 28 The late Jasper Hulley of the One House 1794-1867

Life continued at the One House with Maria Hulley, widow and her four daughters. Ellen married Henry Critchley Broderick MD of Maynes Horse Brigade in 1860. Another daughter Maria – married William Chinner of the Foxhills near Wolverhampton in 1866. This decade was completed by the marriage of Elizabeth to the Revd. Frederick Binley Dickinson at Leamington in July 1869. Ellen and Elizabeth were widowed after only short marriages; Ellen in 1869 and Elizabeth before 1871.

Ellen had married into the Indian Army and had accompanied her husband on a voyage to India, during which time she made daily entries into a diary given to her before departure by her brother Holland Hulley. Henry Critchley Broderick died in Madras in May 1869 and his wife Ellen returned to the One House the following July. The diary provides a fascinating insight, not only into the experiences of the long voyage by sail around the Cape and the shorter route by steam via Suez and Alexandria (the canal was not opened until 5 months later), but also into the life of a major garrison Indian city. It also sheds light on the thoughts and attitudes of an educated Victorian lady, as well as the medical practices of the time.

The One House 1871 census entry[52] consisted of Maria Hulley widow, her stepdaughter Mary and her daughter Sarah Ann, together with 3 servants.

Figure 29 1871 census of the One House

---

[52] RG 10/3571 folio 28 at TNA

Mrs. Hulley was recorded as being at the One House in 1874 and Ellen married her second husband Lieut. Col. J. Durham Hall of the Bombay Staff Corps (2nd Central India Horse) in the same year. The late Mr Howard Chinner of Sevenoaks, Kent owned the diary that covers the period October 1868 to November 1869.

Figure 30 The One House on the 1874 Ordnance Survey map

References -   1507   - Stables & yard   1523   - Kitchen garden
               1508   - The One House   1524, 1525   - Orchard
               1510, 1511   - Gardens, Landscaped

Maria Hulley of the One House died in 1880 and was buried in the family vault in Christ Church, Macclesfield next to her husband, leaving her monies to Sarah Ann and her clothes and jewellery to be divided amongst her remaining children. Sarah Ann married the Rev. Arthur A. Meurant at Windsor in August 1880.

The 1881[53] census shows that Holland and Mary Hulley had moved to Derby by April of that year, and the One House was tenanted by a solicitor – Walter Richard Minor, his wife and four children, two visitors and four servants.

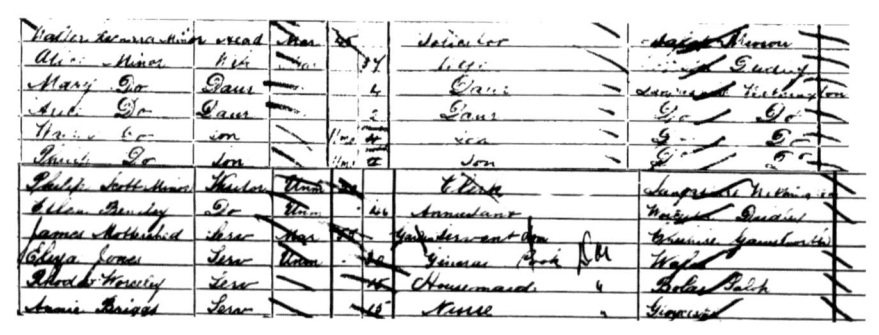

Figure 31 1881 census of the One House

---

[53] RG 11/3490 folios 30 & rev at TNA

The Hulley Coat of Arms

The One House estate now passed to Holland Hulley, who decided to raise the profile of the Hulley family by applying to the College of Arms in London for a Coat of Arms. In 1881 he approached the Cheshire Antiquarian Mr. John P. Earwaker M.A., F.S.A. to research the family's pedigree in preparation to submit a claim to the College. Evidently the family had retained all the copy deeds, surrenders and wills from 1488 to the present time and Earwaker translated all the early Latin documents for use in his researches. From these documents, Earwaker compiled a pedigree and submitted a General Report on the Hulley Pedigree to the College in October 1881. This report is shown at Appendix 7.

Earwaker also extracted all the Hulley, Hooley and Howley entries from St Michael's Church Macclesfield parish registers up to 1756 and copied the entries from the Hulley family bible from 1730 to 1880. Although I had already found many of the details shown in the pedigree, his work assisted in filling in most of the remaining gaps in the story. Thankfully he donated his private papers to the Cheshire Record Office from which much of the material used to write this account is derived. I later found out that copies and counterparts of many of the ancient Hulley papers referred to by Earwaker had been retained by the family whose members emigrated to South Africa around 1860. In 2007, the current head of the family, Mr Jasper Michael Hulley, contacted me to seek my views as to the appropriate location to deposit these papers, which amounted to 271 documents, some written on parchment, some on paper.

I suggested that Cheshire Archives and Local Studies would be pleased to retain them for future access by the public and I brought them back to England after a holiday in South Africa. Before passing them to the Archives, I spent considerable time in cataloging and indexing them to make easy searching. All the details are shown in a 140 page book titled The Hulley Family Papers reference D/392, which is available at the Archives for public consultation, together with all the original documents.

Full details of the Petition and Grant of Arms 1881 are shown at Appendix 8. The Coat of Arms was given to Holland Hulley by the College of Arms and was formally described as follows:

> Sable three Piles Or two issuant from the Chief and one from the Base each charged with a Hillock Vert And for the Crest on a wreath of the Colours A demi-a-mountain reguardant Argent holding between the pairs an Escocheon Or charged with a Hillock Vert, as the same are in the margin hereof more plainly depicted, to be used for ever hereafter by him the said Holland Hulley and his descendants and by the other descendants of his father the said Jasper Hulley deceased, with due and proper differences according to the Laws of Arms.

Coincidentally, the Holland Hulley Coat of Arms bears some identical features of the one granted to John Huley of the City of York as shown in Dugdale's Visitation of 1665. John had originated from Cheshire (as John Hule) in c.1590. His descendants include Sir John Hewley of the City of York.

Figure 32 Coat of Arms of Holland Hulley 1881

(reproduced by kind permission of Mr. Jasper M. Hulley)

The manuscript writing at the bottom reads as follows:

I certify that the above to be the correct Arms and Quarterings of Holland Hulley Esq. of the One House Rainow in co. Chester as they appear upon record in the College of Arms London.   Alfred Scott Gatty Rouge Dragon

Appendix 9 shows the details and origins of the Quarterings on the above Arms.

A 19th Century Ghost

Most ancient houses had their own ghost and the One House was no exception. A regular visitor, Mr Richard E. Knowles, gave an account of the ghost who supposedly haunted the property around the early twentieth century. Writing in 1936, he said that it was nearly 40 years ago since he was told by the then tenant of the One House, an ancient building situated about three miles from Macclesfield, at a hairpin bend in the New Road to Buxton, that a 'ghost' roamed the grounds.

"Even in those days, before the coming of the motor cars and buses, it was a quiet, secluded spot fit for such a tradition, but its position must have been remote before the New Road was made, when the coaches ran straight ahead at Shakespeare's Corner. A stone above the front entrance to the house bears the date 1703, but this merely records its renovation. Shortly after the death of his father, Mr. Arderne Hulley vacated the old home and a succession of tenants lived there, the last of whom before the return of the Hulley family early in the 20th century, I frequently visited and sometimes spent a night."

He mentioned that the hostess (probably Sarah Ann Hulley) had told him that the place was haunted and that it was difficult to keep domestic servants, for they left, giving the excuse that they were too frightened to stop on account of the 'ghost.' He went on to explain that this attitude was probably due to the cabman who drove them up from the railway station in an old four-wheeler. When instructed he would say "You'll not stop there long – the place is haunted." This difficulty was eventually overcome by employing local maids who either did not know of, or were used to the old tradition and did not mind.

The 'ghost' in question was by no means offensive. It took the form of a little old gentleman, dressed in Court clothes, short breeches, silk stockings and shoes with large buckles, who was encountered wandering harmlessly on the drive at night in front of the house or near the stables and outbuildings. On the occasions that Mr. Knowles visited Mr. Arderne Hulley after his return, he never questioned him concerning this apparition, but Mr Knowles went on to recount when he attended a dance at nearby Eddisbury Hall and met Arderne Hulley's daughters and the elderly Miss Hulley. During the interval one of the guests rather scoffingly asked some questions relative to the One House ghost. Miss Hulley was apparently quite annoyed that their 'ghost' should be doubted, and held forth at length as to its authenticity and appearance. He also admitted that neither he nor an old farmer called John Oakes (who lived at Kerridge and was Jasper Hulley's coachman from 1841 until Jasper's death in 1867) had ever seen the alleged ghost. One can speculate that the ghost was the form of one of the previous owners of the One House and there had been plenty to choose from. Narrowing the field down to the older men, was it Jasper who had died in 1867 aged 73? Or was it his grandfather Jasper who died in 1772 aged 76? .

In 1891 the One House Hall (sic) was tenanted by Richard Heaton Smith and his family, as shown in this extract of the census of that year.

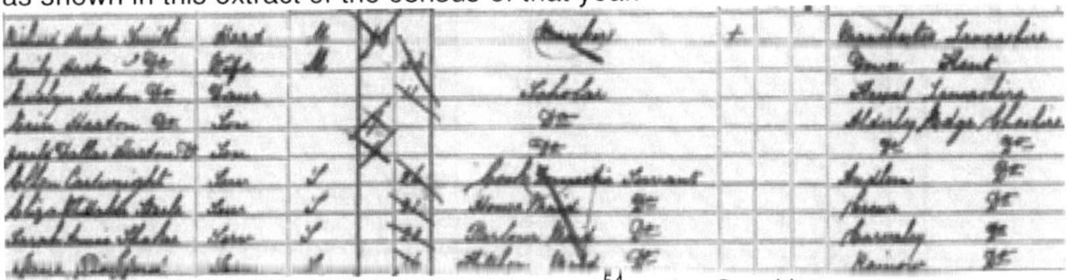

Figure 33 1891 census[54] of the One House

---
[54] RG 12/2811 folio 8 at TNA

6. The Hulley family in the 20th century

The only members of the One House dynasty living in the United Kingdom at the time of the 1901 census were Ellen Hall nee Hulley, the widow of Lieut. Col. J. Durham Hall, and her youngest sister Sarah Ann Meurant, the widow of the Rev. Arthur A. Meurant who she had married in 1880. Both sisters were living together at 31 Brechin Place, Kensington, London, whilst Holland Hulley and his elder sister Mary had moved from Derby and were living near Wolverhampton, presumably to be nearer to the remaining One House family member Maria who had married William Chinner. Although there was no trace of her in 1901, she was listed in the 1911 census, also living near Wolverhampton. Ellen Gorton Hulley, 4th daughter of Arderne Hulley had come to England from her birthplace in Natal, South Africa and was boarding at Woking.

The One House was tenanted by Annie Margarite Gibbons in 1901. She was a widow and lived with her daughter Constance and four servants.

Figure 34 1901 census[55] of the One House

Holland Hulley died in February 1904 and left a limited will with effects of £2,500. Arderne his younger brother took over the family Coat of Arms and returned from South Africa shortly after to inherit the estate. He is mentioned on the Bottfield deeds dated 1905 and on the One House deeds dated 1910. He made a record of his presence in the area in 1911 by inscribing his initials and date on a stile leading from the Lower to the Higher Moor, adjacent to the One House. One wonders whether the stile still exists and whether the inscription A.H. XXVII MAY 1911 is still on it.

Figure 35
The One House on the 1910 Ordnance Survey map. Grove farm is also shown and is 927 feet above sea level.

---

[55] RG 13/3307 folio 9 at TNA

At the time of the 1911 census, the house was solely occupied by a gardener, Frank Jenkinson.

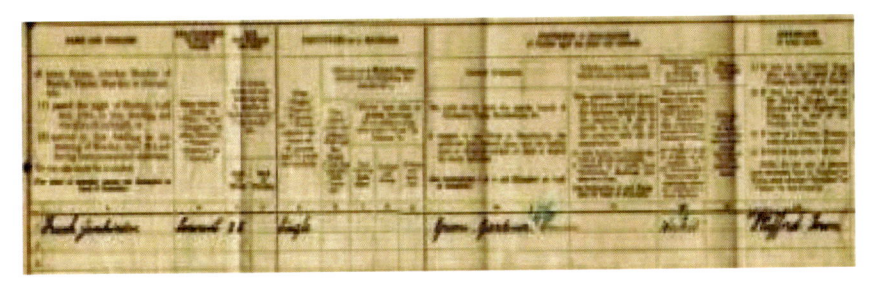

Figure 36 1911 census[56] of the One House

On the 4 December 1912, the One House was surveyed for Inland Revenue purposes to establish an up-to-date Annual Rate for the property. The Board of Inland Revenue Valuation Office Field Books[57] for the Cheadle Hulme sub-district which covers the Rainow Assessments No. 301-355, including the One House, gives a very detailed account of the premises:

331   Situation & RV   One House; £63 (Map 37.5 P)
      Description & Extent House & Garden; 2 acres – now has Knowl Field 3 acres
      Occupier –   Arderne Hulley One House Rainow ½ beneficiary
                                   2 sisters other ½ Mrs Chinner Smestow House Seisdon Nr Dudley; Mrs E. Durham Hall 31 Brechin Place S.Kensington
      Interest of Owner –   Copyhold Manor & Forest of Macclesfield
      Occupier's Tenancy – Yearly; Actual Rent £60; Liable for repairs - Owner
      Who pays (a) Rates & taxes (b) Insurance a – occupier b – owner

Particulars, description, and notes made on inspection (4 Sep 1912)

<u>One House Residence:</u> Built in the 12th Century (Statement of Owner) Quaint design, Situate in its own Grounds & Ornamental Gardens, capital situation, Elevated position, 945ft above sea level, Comprises Entrance Hall, Dining Room, Excellent Drawing Room, Old Drawing or Morning Room, Large Domestic Kitchen & Sculleries, Servant Mans Room, Larders, Pantries, China & Silver Stores, 8 Bedrooms, Drying Room, Bath Room and Smoke Room with Balcony, Lavatory & WC. the place is cellared, Three Stored tower Buildings used for Store, artesian well, supplies at the Residence with wind pump, Four horse Stables, Chop house, Coach house, Saddle Room & Trap Shed. All Stone built Ivy Covered, Grey slated roof. Comfortable Residence in nice order & Repair. Large Kitchen Garden, Quantity of Good trees Chiefly Sycamore Gross Value £1630 10s.

A House (Front rooms) Frontage 100ft x depth 20ft x height 20ft = 40,0000 cu ft (2½)
B   do   (Kitchens &c)   60   37   20 = 44,400
C   do   (Outhouses)   45   23   20 = 20,700   (2)
     Stable   75   20   18 = 27,000   (1¾)
      Timber   £150; Buildings 1070; Total = £1220

---

[56] RG 14/PN21458 at TNA
[57] IR 58/20334 Rainow at TNA

100 Sycamore trees	@ 15/-	75 0 0	
15 Beech	@ 20/-	15 0 0	
10 Ash	@ 30/-	15 0 0	
20 Oak	@ 30/-	30 0 0	
Various Trees	2	20 0 0	Total £155.00

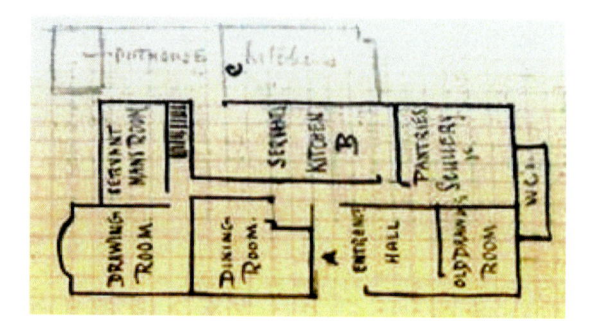

Figure 37 Sketch Plan of the One House in the Inland Revenue Assessment 1912

Sadly this event also signified the end of the Hulley association with the One House because in 1912 the property was sold and the family moved out. Arderne, the last Hulley to live at the One House probably preferred the warmer climate of the south coast to that of Macclesfield (especially after living in South Africa for fifty years) and died in Southsea in 1927 aged 91.

Because the House was such a large one, Brocklehursts the silk manufacturers, who had purchased the property for its water rights, sub-divided it into several flats. The Spering family occupied part of it for two years in 1917-18 and Miss Ethel Buxton lived there between 1925 and 1939. The property was sold in 1938 to Mr T. W. Wood, J.P. of Sutton.

Figure 38 Front left corner of the One House with balcony

Figure 39 A view of the house from the walled garden across the back lane
(Spot the two gardeners!)

An Abode of Gentry

What was the house actually like? The Will of Jonathan Hulley dated 1730 provides an excellent description of his 'goods Cattle Chattels and Effects', by location in the One House. The inventory of the above will reads as follows:

A True and perfect Inventory of the Household goods and other the goods Cattle Chatteles and Effects of Jonathan Hulley late of Rainow in The County of Chester Gentlem: dated Appraized and Vallued the 18" day Of Aug.t 1730

	£ : s : d
Imprs. Goods in the new Kitchen	12 : 12 : 5
Item Goods in the Dining Room	00 : 05 : 0
Item In the Hall	01 : 10 : 0
Item Goods in the Parlor	02 : 03 : 0
Item Goods in the Old Kitchen and Dairy	08 : 04 : 0
Item Goods in the Cellar	02 : 18 : 0
Item Goods in the Cellar Chamber	01 : 13 : 0
Item Goods in the Parlor Chamber	04 : 13 : 0
Item Goods in the Hall Chamber	05 : 00 : 11¼
Item Goods in the New Kitchen Chamber	13 : 01 : 0
Item Goods in the Hall Entry and at Mr Bresties	01 : 02 : 0
Item Goods in the Old Kitchen Chamber	03 : 04 : 4
Item Goods in the Old Kitchen Chamber Loft and New Kitchen Chamber Loft	12 : 08 : 8
Item Goods in the Hall Chamber Loft	21 : 00 : 0
Item Four fatt Oxen A Grey Gelding and Bay Mare	43 : 10 : 0
Item Two Bullocks coming 3 four cow Shirks & two Bullocks Shirks)	18 : 16 : 0
Item A Horse Colt coming 3 A Large Bull & six Calves	16 : 07 : 0
Item Twelve Cows A Twinter Bull & two Heifers	47 : 05 : 0
Item Three Cart Horses A Mare & Fole & four Swine	20 : 10 : 0
Item In husbandry Ware	06 : 14 : 6
Item In Poultry	02 : 05 : 0
Item A Malt mill	00 : 15 : 0
Item In Hay & Corn	48 : 00 : 0
Item In Linen Yame	02 : 08 : 0

Item In Woolen Yarn	00 : 05 : 0
Item In Linens Cloths & Blews, Linens yarns	00 : 11 : 0
Item In Purses & apparills	488: 02 : 8

The goods were appraised by Robert Wild and William Booth and the total valuation came to £755 4s 63/4d. William Booth was one of the deponents in the Jasper Hulley versus Lady Bridget Fauconberg case of 1729.

Other more recent but less detailed accounts of the house come from Miss Buxton, who lived there from 1925 to 1939, in response to an enquiry from an American lady wishing to trace her Hulley ancestry, and Walter Smith, the local historian. Miss Buxton wrote to the Macclesfield Times on 9 December 1965 expressing regret that she did not have a picture of the kitchen window that had 244 9-inch panes of glass. "The kitchen", she added, "would hold four double-deck buses. The magnificent sitting room ceiling was in three panels with hundreds of large and small balls each pegged in separately. Every room had Adam fireplaces and there was a lovely spacious hall with a huge grate. When the paper was removed from this room it revealed that it was painted in oils with water scenes. The building at the back was called The Tower, which was four storeys high, one room on top of the other."

Walter Smith wrote in 1932 about "the spacious apartments and magnificent ceiling of the old dining room, which spoke of the former dignity of this abode of gentry." He also referred to the tower as a "small turret-like semi-detached structure that was said to have been a place where one of the Hulleys confined his wife (or himself, no reliable information can be obtained) for peace and quietness' sake."

Figure 40 A 1920s view of the One House. The tower may be seen at the rear right hand side of the house

Figure 41 View of carriage drive looking towards the front entrance on Buxton Road

Figure 42 View from north west corner looking towards the front right of the One House.

Figure 43 The last Hulley family in the One House. Left to right: Arderne Hulley (1836-1927), his grandson Jasper Robert Arderne Hulley (1910-1990) and his son Jasper Done Clarence Hulley (1877-1935). The photograph was taken in approximately 1911.

The One House Family Tree from 1490 to 1927 is shown at Appendix 10.

Figure 44 This is probably the last known photograph of the One House, a building which had stood on the same spot for over 770 years. The ivy has been cleared from the front façade but the gardener is still tending the garden. It is undated but may be around the early 1930s.

The demise of a 770 year-old house

The One House was finally demolished in August 1939 at the request of the then owner, Mr. G. Brookes. These two exterior shots show the progress of the work by Messrs. Sherratt and Co.

Figures 45, 46 Demolition of the One House - exterior views

Figure 47 This photograph shows the front door with a stone lintel containing the One House Coat of Arms with the motto "One House, One Faith" A.D. 1703 – the year when the house was partially rebuilt by Jonathan Hulley.

The demolition of the house made the local newspaper and the following article appeared in the Macclesfield Times and East Cheshire Observer of the day:

ANCIENT HOUSE DEMOLITION

Queen Reputed To Have Stayed There

THE One House, off Buxton Road, where it is stated, Queen Elizabeth once spent a night when passing through the town, is being demolished and in its place a modern residence is to be erected.

The building and the grounds have been purchased by Mr. G. Brookes, of Upton, Macclesfield, who had hoped to have reconstructed the original house. This was found impossible and for the past few weeks Messrs. Sherratt and Co. have been busily engaged in demolishing it.

The One House was one of the oldest residences in Macclesfield and a stone above the main entrance bore the inscription "Re-built 1703."

Mr. Sherratt of the firm engaged in the demolition work, told a "Macclesfield Times" reporter that the new owner had hoped to save parts of the building, but this had been found impossible owing to its great age. The woodwork, he said, was rotten and some of the stones crumbled when disturbed. Some of the walls were three feet thick and, in the centre, plastic made of mud and twigs has been discovered.

"We found an underground passage," said Mr. Sherratt," and whilst we do not know to where this originally led I am of the opinion that it was probably part of a passage going to the Parish Church. A few years ago when some property was being demolished at the rear of the Parish Church an underground passage was discovered there and this went in the direction of Buxton Road. Whether there was any connection between the two passages I do not know.

"I understand that the One House was originally built by a Mr. Savage, whose family were associated with the Parish Church.

"Mr. Brookes wanted the large stone over the main doorway, bearing the inscription 'Rebuilt 1703' saving, but it crumbled when we took it down."

Mr. Brookes is to build a new residence on the original site of the One House and as many of the stones as possible will be utilised.

Figure 48 Newspaper article – Ancient House Demolition

The reference in the article to an underground passage was probably the cellars of a building on the site that had been demolished long before the current work. The inscription read "A.D. 1703" and was contained inside some kind of a shield. Although the One House family crest was not in existence at that time, it must have been added later.

The final postscript to this newspaper report is shown on the same page of the "Times" as the above story. This is a small, perhaps pathetic, advertisement that reads:

STONE RUBBLE FREE FOR CARTING.—APPLY ONE HOUSE, BUXTON ROAD or 18 BRUNSWICK SQUARE, SHERRATT AND SON.

Figure 49 Newspaper advert – Stone Rubble

For some unknown reason the proposal to build a new house was not adopted and the site has remained more or less as the demolishers left it over 75 years ago.

A Mr. Cunningham who lived near the One House and was studying for his 'O' level History qualification in c.1985, wrote a Project Report entitled 'The One House or Manor House of Rainow' which he kindly copied to me. He interviewed several members of the local community as well as people who once lived at the house and his report contained much useful information. A copy is available at the local library.

Although the One House and its families are no longer in Rainow, there are still Hulleys and Hooleys living in the area today, mainly the direct descendants of James, son of Jasper Howley who was born in 1625, and who inherited the One House on the death of his father John in 1676. James founded the Macclesfield Forest family tree – shown at reference Ches04 in website www.hulley.info – whose descendants are amongst those mentioned above.

I have established a DNA project and the results from two of the members prove conclusively that they are descendants of the One House family. One with a Hulley surname is a descendant of the Hulley/Hooley families of Macclesfield Forest (Ches04) whose lead person – James Howley b1679 – was the youngest son of Jasper Howley (1625-1700) of the One House. The other has a Hooley surname and has an almost identical DNA match with the Hulley above, and clearly is a close relative in the distant past. Unfortunately his particular family tree – shown in Ches15 – ends at a James Hooley who was the father of James Hooley born in 1828. So although documentary evidence to support his relationship is currently wanting, the DNA evidence is conclusive.

What is my own connection with the Hulley families of the One House? Apart from writing this account, I have found no direct link with the families who lived there and although my 37 marker DNA matches that of the One House family in 29 markers, this indicates that there is no close link between the two family trees. My own ancestors come from Ashton under Lyne and Dukinfield. The adjacent hamlet of Hooley Hill is almost certainly named after John Hooley who was Constable of Dukinfeld in 1514 and is shown on the Lay Subsidy Roll of 1546. Although my own family tree shares common first names e.g. Lawrence and John with the One House tree, the only indirect link so far established is shown in the 1668 will of Miles Howley of Adlington, possibly a distant branch of the One House family. He appointed Peter Mottram of Adlington and William Howley of Dukinfield as his executors. Unfortunately the relationship between Miles and William is not given and the absence of DNA evidence from a male descendant of the Howley family of Adlington is a barrier to further research.

Figure 50 Hulley documents from South Africa prior to sorting and indexing.

Figure 51 The front entrance to the One House on Buxton Road

Figure 52 The ornate front gate of the One House – now replaced.

Figure 53 The author's wife Joan at the One House rear gate.

Figure 54 The view from the One House towards Macclesfield

Appendix 1 Supporting Documents 1290 – 1348

D1. The Manor of One House

English transcription from the original Latin by John Earwaker, Cheshire Historian when researching the Hulley pedigree for the granting of Arms in 1881 to Holland Hulley.

Be it known to all that I RICHARD DE LEGGES have given, granted, and absolutely, for me and my heirs or assigns for ever, quit claimed, to ROBERT son of ROBERT DE RODE and his heirs or assigns, all my right which I have or can claim in all the lands and tenements of Honhuss, (*One House*) without anything retaining for ever as freely quietly, rightly, and hereditarily, as I RICHARD DE LEGGES and my feoffees have held or should hold the said tenements so that neither I RICHARD DE LEGGES nor my heirs and assigns, nor any in my name or on my part shall have any right or claim on the aforesaid lands and tenements for ever   In testimony of which thing to these presents my seal is affixed

These being Witnesses
GNONE DE FULTON, now Bailiff
ROBERT DE DOUNES,
RICHARD DE SUTTON
ADAM BIRAN
JOHN DE ASTBURY
WILLIAM DE HURDESFIELD
THOMAS the CLERK
and others

(Not dated – seal gone) Estimated date 1290 - 1300 (Richard de Legg, Adam de Biran, John de Astbury and Thomas the Clerk were all witnesses during this period.)

Source – Davenport Deeds Capesthorne

D2. Grant from THOMAS son and heir of ROBERT DE RODE to ADAM son of ADAM DE ASTUL of all his lands &c in Honhuss *(One House)* in the Forest of Macclesfield

English transcription from the original Latin by John Earwaker Cheshire Historian when researching the Hulley pedigree for the granting of Arms in 1881 to Holland Hulley.

Let present and future know that I THOMAS son and heir of ROBERT DE RODE have given and granted and by this my present charter confirmed to ADAM son of ADAM DE ASTUL his heirs and assigns, all my lands and my tenements in Honhuss in the Forest of Macclesfield, with all their appurtenances nothing retaining to have and to hold of the Chief Lord of the fee in such free and quiet manner as I and my predecessors have held or should hold the same for ever – yielding therefor yearly, and rendering to the Chief Lord the service due and accustomed – And I the said THOMAS and my heirs and assigns all the aforesaid lands and tenements with all their appurtenances, to the said ADAM his heirs and assigns, against all mortals for ever, will warrant, acquit and defend – In testimony of which thing to this present charter I have placed my seal in my full and lawful power and age.

These being Witnesses

JORDEIN DE MACCLESFIELD now Bailiff
JOHN DE SUTTON
EDMUND DE DOWNES
JOHN DE BOUSDEN
WILLIAM the Clerk
and others

Estimated date 1326 - 1330 (Jordan de Macclesfield was Bailiff 1326 - 1331)

Source – Davenport Deeds Capesthorne

****

D3. Grant from ADAM son of ADAM DE ASTHULL to JOHN son of THOMAS DE DAVENPORT and MARGERY his wife of all his lands &c in On hous *(One House)* in the Forest of Macclesfield

English transcription from the original Latin by John Earwaker, Cheshire Historian when researching the Hulley pedigree for the granting of Arms in 1881 to Holland Hulley.

Let present and future know that I ADAM son of ADAM DE ASTHULL have given, granted, and by this my present charter confirmed to JOHN son of THOMAS DE DAVENPORT and MARGERY his wife and my land and tenements with their appurtenances in Onhous in the Forest of Macclesfield – To hold and to have to the aforesaid JOHN and MARGERY and their heirs, of the Chief Lords of the fee by the service which belongs to these tenements for ever, freely, quietly well and in peace, with all liberties, freedoms, customs, improvements, commons and easements, which to those tenements in any manner shall belong. And I the aforesaid ADAM son of ADAM DE ASTHULL and my heirs all the aforesaid lands and tenements with their appurtenances to the aforesaid JOHN & MARGERY and their heirs against all people will warrant, acquit and defend. In testimony of which thing to this my present charter, I have placed my seal.

These being Witnesses
WILLIAM DE BURTIN, Knight
JORDAN DE MACCLESFELD
THOMAS DE DAVENPORT
ROGER DE MORTLOWE
EDMUND DE DOUNES
JOHN DE SUTTON
THOMAS DE SLADEHURD
and others

Given at Macclesfield on Tuesday on the feast of the translation of St. Thomas the Martyr *(7 July)* 5 Edward III *(1331)*

Seal gone

Source – Davenport Deeds Capesthorne

****

D4. Feoffment from SIR JOHN DE DAVENPORT, Knt., to JOHN DE PASSELEGH and WILLIAM DE WELDON, chaplains, of all his lands &c at Onhous (One House), in Hurdsfield &c.

English transcription from the original Latin by John Earwaker, Cheshire Historian when researching the Hulley pedigree for the granting of Arms in 1881 to Holland Hulley.

Let present and future know that I JOHN DE DAVENPORT Knight have given, granted, and by this my present charter confirmed to JOHN DE PASSELEGH and WILLIAM DE WELDON, chaplains, their heirs and assigns all my lands and tenements with all their appurtenances at On hous in the vill of Hurdesfield – And also all my lands and Tenements with all their appurtenances which HAMMOT DE TURNOK and ROBERT DE SAKESTON hold for a term of years of me in the vill of Withinton by Marton - And also all those my lands and tenements with all their appurtenances which HENRY RUGH formerly held of me for a term of years, Together with all those wastes with their appurtenances which I had of the gift and feoffment of ROGER DE DAVENPORT of SOMERFORD, my brother in the same vill of Withinton – to have and to hold to the aforesaid JOHN and WILLIAM their heirs and assigns all the aforesaid lands and tenements and wastes with all their appurtenances therein and gardens, freely, quietly, well and in peace for ever, with all commons, liberties and easements to the aforesaid Lands and tenements in any manner belonging of the Chief Lord of that fee, by service therefor due and accustomed.

And I the aforesaid JOHN DE DAVENPORT Knight and my heirs, all the aforesaid Lands and Tenements and wastes with all their appurtenances to the aforesaid JOHN DE PASSELEGH and WILLIAM DE WELDON chaplains, their heirs and assigns against all people will warrant and for ever defend – In testimony of which thing to this my present charter I have placed my seal.

These being Witnesses
ROBERT DE LEGH
JOHN DE BOSDON
JOHN DE SUTTON
THOMAS DE DAVENPORT of the Trustede
JOHN LE BARKERAILE
RICHARD LE WARDE of Somerford
and others

Given at Merton in the Hundred of Macclesfield on Sunday next after the feast of St Fabian and Sebastian *(20 Jan)* 20 Edward III *(1346-47)*

Source – Davenport Deeds Capesthorne

Footnote – there was a WILLIAM DF WELDON Vicar of Sandbach before 1347 in which year he died.

****

D5. Quitclaim from HAWISE widow of ADAM de Honhouse to JOHN DE PASSELEGH and WILLIAM DE WILDON Chaplains, of all her right in the lands &c of Honhouse *(One House)* in the Forest of Macclesfield

English transcription from the original Latin by John Earwaker, Cheshire Historian when researching the Hulley pedigree for the granting of Arms in 1881 to Holland Hulley.

Be it known to all by these presents that I HAWISE who was the wife of ADAM DE HONHOUSE have remised, released and absolutely for me and my heirs quit-claimed to JOHN DE PASSELEGH and WILLIAM DE WELDON Chaplains, all my right and claim which I have or shall in all the Lands and Tenements with their appurtenances of Honhouse within the Forest of Macclesfield – so that I the said HAWISE, nor my heirs shall have any right to claim in the aforesaid lands and tenements, but therefrom shall be excluded for ever. And I the said HAWISE and my heirs acqt the aforesaid lands and tenements with their appurtenances to the aforesaid JOHN and WILLIAM their heirs and assigns against all people, will warrant and for ever – in testimony of which thing, to the present writing I have placed my seal.

These being Witnesses
JORDAN DE MACCLESFELD
JOHN DE BOSDEN
JOHN DE SUTTON
JOHN son of RICHARD DE SUTTON
and others

Given at "On house" on Saturday next after the feast of All Saints *(1 Nov)* in the 21st year of the reign of King Edward the Third after the Conquest *(1347)*

Source – Davenport Deeds Capesthorne

****

Additional information about John Hulley

A further development in the John Hulley of Liverpool story is the erecting of a statue to his memory on Liverpool waterfront in June 2019. The statue was unveiled by her Royal Highness the Princess Royal, Princess Anne.

There are two videos on YouTube that covered the unveiling ceremony –

[John Hulley Statue Unveiled by Princess Anne in Liverpool](#)

[The Road to John Hulley 2019](#)

I hope that you will enjoy watching them! Full details of the life of John Hulley is at www.johnhulley-olympics.co.uk

D6. Grant of the Manor of One House in the Forest of Macclesfield &c from JOHN DE PASSELEGH and WILLIAM DE WELDON, Chaplains to SIR JOHN DE DAVENPORT, Knt., and MARGERY his wife

English transcription from the original Latin by John Earwaker, Cheshire Historian when researching the Hulley pedigree for the granting of Arms in 1881 to Holland Hulley.

Let present and future know that we JOHN DE PASSELEGH and WILLIAM DE WELDON Chaplains, have given, granted and by this my present charter, confirmed to JOHN DE DAVENPORT, Knight, and MARGERY his wife, our Manor of On Hous with its appurtenances in the Forest of Macclesfield, and also all our messuages lands and tenements with their appurtenances which HAMNET DE TURNOGH, RICHARD ADAMESONE, and HENRY LOKET, hold of us for a term of years, between the vill of Sydington and a certain watercourse which extends from Kocshawemarsche in the vill of Wythinton by Marton as far as the land of THOMAS DE BROMALE, and so descending to Peuer Hel – To have and to hold to the aforesaid JOHN and MARGERY, freely, quietly, well, and in peace, of The Chief Lords of that fee by the service therefor due, and accustomed for the term of the lives of them the said JOHN and MARGERY, with all their appurtenances also we will and grant that after the decease of the said JOHN and MARGERY the aforesaid Manor of On house and all the messuages, lands, tenements aforesaid with their appurtenances shall wholly remain to JOHN son of the said JOHN and MARGERY, and the heirs male of his body issuing to hold of the Chief Lords of that fee by the service therefor due and accustomed – And if it happens that the aforesaid JOHN shall die without heir male of his body issuing, then we will and grant that the aforesaid Manor and all the messuages, lands, tenements aforesaid with their appurtenances shall wholly remain to RICHARD son of the said JOHN and MARGERY, and the heirs male of his body issuing to hold of the Chief Lords of that fee by the service therefor due and accustomed – And if it happens that the aforesaid RICHARD shall die without heir male of his body issuing, then we will and grant that the aforesaid Manor and all the messuages, lands, tenements aforesaid with their appurtenances shall wholly remain to ROGER and ARTHUR sons of the said JOHN and MARGERY, and the heirs male of his body issuing to hold of the Chief Lords of that fee by the service therefor due and accustomed – And it it happens that and if the aforesaid ROGER and ARTHUR shall die without heir male of their bodies issuing, then we will and grant that the aforesaid Manor and all the messuages, lands, tenements aforesaid with their appurtenances shall wholly remain to the right heirs of the aforesaid JOHN DE DAVENPORT Knight to hold of the Chief Lords of that fee by the service which belongs to the aforesaid tenements for ever.

And we truly the aforesaid JOHN DE PASSELEGH and WILLIAM DE WELDON Chaplains, and our heirs, the aforesaid Manor and all the messuages, lands, tenements aforesaid with their appurtenances to the aforesaid JOHN DE DAVENPORT Knight and MARGERY his wife for their lives and after the decease of the said JOHN and MARGERY then to JOHN son of the said JOHN and MARGERY, and the heirs male of his body issuing and if the aforesaid JOHN shall die without heirs male of his body, then to the aforesaid RICHARD son of the said JOHN and MARGERY, and the heirs male of his body and if the aforesaid RICHARD shall die without heirs male of his body, then to the aforesaid ROGER and ARTHUR and the heirs male of their bodies, and if the aforesaid ROGER and ARTHUR shall die without heirs male of their bodies then to the right heirs of the aforesaid JOHN DE DAVENPORT Knight with warrant, acquit and ever defend.

In Testimony of which thing to this our present charter we have placed our seals.
These being Witnesses
THOMAS DE DAVENPORT
JOHN DE BAICRENILE
RANDLE DE SWETENHAM
RICHARD DE SOMERFORD
RICHARD LE WARK OF SOMERFORD and others

Given at Withinton by Marton on Friday next (11 January) after the Epiphany of our Lord A.D 1348
Seal of red brown wax not heraldic and fragment of the other seal.

Source – Davenport Deeds Capesthorne

Appendix 2 Owners and/or tenants of the One House

Date/Period	Person	Information	Source
1153 - 1181	Richard de Davenport	Appointed supreme forester by Earl Hugh of Cyveilig [1208-1211] - given a place in the Hundred of Macclesfield, by the service of forestry, in free and hereditary called 'ANHUS'.	J.R.U.L.M. Bromley-Davenport Muniments, Deeds, Davenports of Davenport (i)
bef. 1205 - aft. 1254	Vivian de Davenport	Richard's successor (poss. born bef. 1190) - granted office of master serjeant of Macclesfield [1216-1226], died by 1260.	The Early History of the Davenports of Davenport Auth. T.P. Highet; Pub. Chetham Society Series 3 Volume 9 p4 1960
bef. 1290	Richard de Legges	Granted Honhuss tenancy to Robert de Rode in 1290-1300.	Grant est. date 1290-1300; Davenport Deeds Capesthorne; copy at Appendix 1 D1.
up to 1291-96	Roger de Davenport	Eldest son of Vivian de Davenport mar. Mary Salemon [d. 1301]	The Early History of the Davenports of Davenport Auth. T.P. Highet; Pub. Chetham Society Series 3 Volume 9 p4 1960
bef. 1290	Robert de Rode	Son of Robert de Rode – granted Honhuss tenancy.	Grant est. date 1290-1300; Davenport Deeds Capesthorne; copy at Appendix 1 D1.
up to 1320	Thomas de Davenport	[c1260-c1320] Successor to Roger, acting serjeant of the peace mar. Agnes of Macclesfield	The Early History of the Davenports of Davenport Auth. T.P. Highet; Pub. Chetham Society Series 3 Volume 9 p4 1960
c1326	Thomas de Rode	Son of Robert de Rode - granted tenancy of the One House	Grant est. date 1326-1330; Davenport Deeds Capesthorne; copy at Appendix 1 D2.
bef. 1331	Adam de Astul	Son of Adam de Astul - granted tenancy by Thomas de Rode	Grant est. date 1326-1330; Davenport Deeds Capesthorne; copy at Appendix 1 D2.
7 Jul 1331	John de Davenport & Margery his wife	[c.1288-1358] Successor to Thomas; married Margery de Brereton; granted Onhous tenancy by Adam de Asthull.	Grant dated 7 Jul 1331, Davenport Deeds Capesthorne; copy at Appendix 1 D3.
20 Jan 1346-47	John de Passelegh & William de Weldon	(Chaplains to Sir John Davenport Kt.), Granted On hous tenancy by John de Davenport Knight	Grant dated 20 Jan 1346-47; Davenport Deeds Capesthorne; copy at Appendix 1 D4.

Date/Period	Person	Information	Source
1 Nov 1347	Hawise de Astul	Wife of Adam of Honhouse surrendered al her rights to Honhouse	Quitclaim 1 Nov 1347; Davenport Deeds Capesthorne; copy at Appendix 1 D5.
11 Jan 1348	John de Davenport Kt. & Margery his wife	[c1288-1358] Granted On Hous tenancy by John de Passelegh and William de Waldon	Grant dated 11 Jan 1348, Davenport Deeds Capesthorne; copy at Appendix 1 D6.
1358	John de Davenport	Successor to John de Davenport Kt. Granted On Hous tenancy	Grant dated 11 Jan 1348, Davenport Deeds Capesthorne; copy at Appendix 1 D6.
no date	Richarde Davenport	Successor to John de Davenport. Granted On Hous tenancy	Grant dated 11 Jan 1348, Davenport Deeds Capesthorne; copy at Appendix 1 D6.
no date	Roger de Davenport	Successor to Richard de Davenport. Granted On Hous tenancy	Grant dated 11 Jan 1348, Davenport Deeds Capesthorne; copy at Appendix 1 D6.
no date	Arthur de Davenport	Successor to Roger de Davenport. Granted On Hous tenancy married Katherine de Calveley; killed at the battle of Shrewsbury 1403 whilst supporting Richard II	Grant dated 11 Jan 1348, Davenport Deeds Capesthorne; copy at Appendix 1 D6. See also IPM 1394; A history & genealogy of the Davenport family of England and America; Author - Davenport A. B. Pub S. Benedict New York 1851 p56.
1403	Henry Davenport	Son of Arthur married Isabella had issue Arthur who died before his father.	A history and genealogy of the Davenport family of England and America ;Author - Davenport A. B. Pub. S. Benedict New York 1851 p56.
no date	Arthur Davenport	Son of Henry married Margery but died before his father	Margery 'late wife to Arthur Davenport' One House lease 1490; copy at Appendix 3.
bef. 1490	Rauf Davenport	Successor of Arthur Davenport	'Rauf Davernporte of Calveley' One House lease dated 1490; copy at Appendix 3.
bef. 1490	Hugh Davenport	Son of Rauf Davenport	High Davenport son & heyre of Rauf' lease dated 1490; copy at Appendix 3.
2 Mar 1490	Rauf Davenport of Calveley and son Hugh	Made an Indenture to 'set and let to farme to the said John Hulley a parcel of land poell of lond cald one howse lyinge in Raynowe'.	One House lease dated 1490; copy at Appendix 3.
after 2 Mar 1490	John Hulley	With Alic my wyfe and my childr lafulle begettyn Lawrans and Ellyn and M'get and Annes	One House lease dated 1490; copy at Appendix 3; Deed by John Hulley of the nature of a Will c. 1500

Appendix 3 Lease of the One House dated 1490

Front of lease

THIS indenture made the ijde day of March the Vth yere of the Reign of Kyng Henre the VIJth [*1490*] Betwene **Rauf Davernporte** of Calveley and **Hugh Davernport** son and heyre apparent of the said **Rauf** opon that one ptie, And **John Hulley** opon that other ptie Witnesseth that the sayd **Rauf & Hugh** have set and let to farme to the said **John Hulley** a pcell of lond cald one howse lyinge in Raynowe wt. The apptenncez [*appurtenances*] to have and to holde the said pcell of lond cald on howse wth. Thapptenncez to the said **John** & his assygnes durynge the terme of xlv yerez next ensuying aftr the decesse of **Margere** late wyf to **Arthur Davernporte** yeldinge therefore yerely to the said **Rauf** & to his heyrez xxs.xxd at the festez of the Natyultie of Saint John Bapt and Saint Martyn in Wyntr by evyn porconz or wt in xxte days ayther of the said fests next suyinge. And to the chefe lord of the fee the Rent therof due & accustomed and yf the said Rent be byhynd at other of the said fests yt it ogh [*ought*] to be paid by xxte days the said fests next suying [*ensuing*]. Then it shalbe lawfull to the said **Rauf** and his heyrez on the said lond to distresse and the distresses so taken to dryf and Cary away & anends [*against*] theym to hold unto the tyme yt thay be content & satisfied of the said rent & the arrerages [*arrears*] yt of and if the said rent be byhynd unpaid at other of the saidz fests yt it ogh to be paid at by a quartr of a yere the said fests next suying and no sufficient distresse may be fond in the said lond then it shalbe laghfull [*lawful*] to the said **Rauf** & to his heyrez in to the said lond to reentre & hit in theyre furst estate to hold this indenture in any Wyse not Wythstondyng Also **the said John Hulley** graunts by these presents yt he shall do covenable s'vyce [*service*] to **Rog. Legh** of the Rege [*Ridge*] reservyng hs maistere   Also the saids **Rauf & Hugh** graunten by these presents yt they or other of theym shall make an estate to the said **John** of the said lond by byll indented wtin a qrtr of a yere next ensuying aftr the decesse of the said **Marge** fore teme of the said yeres yeldynge yt fore yerely to the said **Rauf** & to his heyrez the rent above reherset.   In Witnesse wherof to these presents the said pties entrchaungeable have putt theyre sealz   Gevyn the day and yere reherset.

Reverse of lease

       Apud on howse iiij die Aprilis
       Ao dmi 1568 pastures conteyning to the same as followeth

1. Impris   on pasture called the feild at the close
2. Itm   on other pasture called the myddle field
3. Itm   on other called the lower field
4. Itm   on other called the barr field
5. Itm   on other called the walle field
   Itm   on small close lying to daye ?beeky?

1489-90

(John Hulley inherited the One House from Lawrence his father on 26 Dec 1566)

Appendix 4 Deed by John Hulley of the nature of a Will c. 1500

THIS Writyng beyrys wyttenes yt I **John Hulley** leves *[leaves]* a howse and a *nacre [an acre]* of lond, and a grond ye gweche *[which]* ys called on howse lyynge in ye town of Rawnae & the gwech yt I have takyn to ye tyme of v & xl zere next folowyng aftr ye desesse of Marg'e yt was ye wyfe of Arthur Davemport of Calveley aftr. Her dissesse to me **John Hulley** and to myne assigns after myn desesse to **Alic my wyfe** and to **my childr** lafulle begettyn to **lawrans** & to **Ellyn** and **M'get** And **Annes** for to be Ann'seers *[overseers]* of this lond **Jamg Hulley my brodr.** And **Richard** and **Willia** and **Hug** that they shall see yt my howse and a nacre of lond lyynge to hit be up holdyn and keppet as hit shuld be also ye tacke of ye lond wt ye wode yt yes *[these]* my sectures *[executors]* syn see yt hit be ockepiet to ye most p'fet of ye lond. Also I will yt **Alic my wyfe** have hit As long as she kepys my name and also as long as thes my sectures thinke yt she ockepyes as they thinke a shuld doe to ye behofe of hir and my childur.

I **John Hulley** make sectures and seners *[executors and overseers]* **James Hulley Ric. Hulley Willia Hulley** and Hug Hulley and **Alice my wyfe** And **my childr** put them in strenketh of covans made betwyx Rafe Davemport And Hug ye son of ye sayd Rafe and heyr of pairand *[apparent]* of Calveley And Above namet John on ye todr *[the other]* parte And yt ye sayd John with Alic his wyfe and his childr And aftr them ye Aldest secutore next foloyng yt they may have all grantes and cov'andes maket by twene Rafe Davemport and Hug his son on ye tonparte *[the one]* and ye said **John** on ye todr parte witt yt all mangrantes and cou'andes be to ye behofe of **Alic** my wif And my childr And to ye secutoresse *[executors]* afore reherset yt yey be my neyrs *[mine heirs]* And myn Asenesse *[assigns]* And myn ..... all grantes & cou'andis yt be made betwixt ye sayd Raf upon ye one parte **John** above said on ye odr pte I will yt yis writyng be myn attorney.

Appendix 5 Background Notes to the 1757 Church Dispute

By John P. Earwaker

About 150 years ago all or most of the Lands afterwards divided into the Townships of Hurdsfield, Kettleshulme, Pott Shrigley, Bollington, Disley Stanley, Waley, Wildboarclough, Winkle & Sutton were unenclosed Common grounds within the Manor of Macclesfield belonging to and afterwards purchased from the Crown, and the said purchasers and owners thereof are now Tenants of the Crown and the Township of Macclesfield Forest was the King's Forest afterwards granted to the Earl of Derby, and all lies within the Parish of Prestbury.

About 100 or 200 years since Macclesfield Borough an ancient Corporation was a poor town in the Parish of Prestbury and had a small Chapel of Ease then in very bad order & the Steeple and Spire or Obelisk were so dangerous to the inhabitants of Macclesfield then (all or most of therein Tenants or Copyholders under the Crown) so few in number that they applied to the neighbouring country Townships in the parish that lay remotest from the Parish of Prestbury, namely Lyme Handley, Pott Shrigley, Kettleshulme, Hurdsfield, Rainow, Sutton, Macclesfield Forest, Wildboarclough, and Winkle to assist them to build a new steeple and to repair and re-timber part of the Chapel and there being no Chapel in Rainow, Winkle, or Macclesfield Forest, which are each 4 or 5 miles from the Parish Church of Prestbury.

The said Townships contributed not only to build the steeple but to keep the Chapel of Macclesfield in repair and so continued to do so for several years; but Lyme Handley and some parts of Shrigley being all Legh tenants many years ago withheld their share and the other Townships continued their payments and the usual rate generally collected yearly was £54 of which the inhabitants of Macclesfield paid £18; Wincle, Wildboarclough, Sutton, Macclesfield Forest £18 amongst them; and Pott Shrigley, Kettleshulme, Rainow and Hurdsfield the other £18 amongst them. And one of the Wardens for the said Chapel were yearly chosen out of some of the said Townships in their turn and saw how the money so collected was applied; but for upwards of 30 years past the people of Macclesfield have refused to suffer any of the inhabitants of the other Townships to be Wardens or to intermeddle or be concerned in the application of the money collected. And many charities have been given which are yearly distributed and the Sacrament for many years has been monthly administered and all this charitable Benefactions and all the offering money, have been distributed among the poor of Macclesfield only and no part of either to any of the poor of the other Townships. Notwithstanding these proceedings the said yearly rates were collected, and freely paid towards keeping the said Chapel in repair until some years last past when it appeared that the money was converted and applied to feasting and other uses quite different to what was only intended.

The Town of Macclesfield for some years has been mightily increased, and is become so populous that the said Chapel was too small to contain the inhabitants of its own Township of Macclesfield and the inhabitants of Macclesfield in 1737 applied for a Writ and afterwards did take down a side of the said Chapel and have built one near being as large as it was before without consulting or advising with the said Townships to the charge of which the above Townships (contributed as aforesaid very little) but the said Chapel tho' so much enlarged is still too small even for the inhabitants of the said Township of Macclesfield itself. Nor is there any seats or room for any of the inhabitants of the above mentioned Townships to sit in except a very few which some of the inhabitants of the said Townships have purchased. For these reasons several of the said Townships have built Chapels of their own for Divine Worship, and keep and maintain preaching Ministers at their own expense. In Winkle 1 Chapel, Pott Shrigley 1 Chapel, Lyme Handley 1 Chapel, Macclesfield Forest 1 Chapel, Rainow 2 Chapels. And several years since Mr. Legh's Tenants of his several farms in Lyme Handley and Kettleshulme withheld their payments and note the inhabitants of Macclesfield Forest, tenants to Lord Derby allege that their share was paid in case of Sutton for a certain term only and refuse to continue it. And the inhabitants of Wildboarclough, also tenants to Lord Derby allege that their share was paid in case of Winkle, for a term of years only and refuse to continue (since the money as they think hath been misapplied). And the inhabitants of rest of the said Townships hope they are and maybe exempted from paying any longer to the Chapel of Macclesfield since Lyme Handley has many years refused to pay any more and Mr. Legh's tenants in Kettleshulme refused and are excused from paying their share and the inhabitants of Macclesfield Forest, and of Wildboarclough all Lord Derby's tenants refuse to pay their share, and the Macclesfield people have refused to let any of the other inhabitants be Wardens, and have for the use of their own Town made a Chapel so much larger and without the joint consent of the rest of the Townships and refuse to bestow any of the offering or charity money on any or the poor inhabitants of the other Townships and apply the money collected by the rates to uses besides repairing the said Chapel; and the other Townships pay to their Mother Church of Prestbury and their own respective Chapels.

Note.
The Mayor of the Corporation of Macclesfield has and always had the power in himself to nominate the Prime Minister and the inhabitants of Macclesfield or the Mayor and Aldermen choose the Curate and *[illegible]* his wages till about 2 years ago or something more. The Wardens of Macclesfield paid the Curate five pounds a year out of the Chappelry as an addition to his salary without ever making the Townships' acquaintance with it.

Appendix 6 Correspondence - Colours of "Hulley's Volunteers" 1912

The fate of the Colours 110 years after they had been raised was the subject of correspondence in the Macclesfield Courier and Herald in October 1912.

A VALUABLE RELIC

To the Editor of the Macclesfield Courier
Dear Sir, - Over a century ago two regiments of Volunteers were embodied in Macclesfield to defend our native land against the invasion at that time threatened by Bonaparte. These regiments were respectively called "The Macclesfield Loyal Foresters" and the "Loyal Macclesfield Volunteer Infantry."
Their flags were preserved for many years in the Old Church. They are still in existence, and although they are old and worn and dilapidated, they are of great historical interest and value. One flag is dark blue silk with the Royal Arms in the centre, and the other is of crimson silk with the Union Jack in the left-hand corner. In the centre is a wreath of oak leaves and acorns, and it has on it the Arms of the Borough of Macclesfield and the motto "Nec cupia nec virtus desunt." (*Neither virtue nor plenty are lacking*). I am informed by Mr. Wm. Trotter, estate agent, etc., that these two flags are in his possession, having been entrusted to him by Mr. Hulley, late of the One House, Buxton Road.

May I respectfully suggest that these ancient historical relics of Macclesfield's loyalty and patriotism during a time of national peril ought to be preserved in one of our public institutions. I believe that Mr. Trotter would be pleased to deliver them up to any duly authorised persons with a view to their preservation in some public building, such as the Park Museum or the Old Church.
        Yours sincerely,
                JOHN EARLES
[We suggest that our esteemed correspondent should call the personal attention of his Worship the Mayor to the facts disclosed in his letter above. - Ed. "M.C. & H."]

(*1911 census – William Trotter aged 46 born Buglawton, Cheshire; Estate Agent of 80 Derby Street, Macclesfield; John Earles aged 50 born Macclesfield, Cheshire; Elementary School Teacher 47 Byrons Lane Macclesfield*)

****

MACCLESFIELD IN THE DAYS OF BONAPARTE.

To the Editor of the Macclesfield Courier

Dear Sir. - I am pleased to learn that the colours of the old Macclesfield Volunteers are still in existence.

In boyhood they were objects of great interest to me as they hung, tattered, faded, and dust-laden from the walls of the Old Church. I was then not cognizant of their history, and imagination invested them with a charm and dignity even greater perhaps than was their due; for I loved to think of them as having braved both the battle and the breeze, and that they were shot-riddled and war-stained in active service. Doubtless it was but from lack of opportunity that their history was but a peaceful one, for stout hearts beat in the bosoms of our forefathers in the days when the first Napoleon cast his covetous glances towards our tight little island and the men who gathered round these flags would not have disgraced the land of their birth, had they been called upon to fight in its defence.

Why were these colours removed from the Church during the restoration of 1883?

They were deposited in the sacred edifice with solemn rite and ceremony when the corps were disbanded and I question the action of those in authority in 1883. My recollection of the disposal is that it was said that the colours were so dilapidated as to be unfit for re-hanging. But the fact that they are in existence today, thirty years after their removal, disproves this statement.

I most respectfully suggest that it would be a graceful act for the present possessors to offer to restore the historic emblems to the custodianship of the Church from which they were then removed. They are a connecting link with civic life in the very early days of the nineteenth century and, though they have doubtless been carefully treasured for family reasons in the home of the Hulleys, of the One House (for which the grateful thanks of the community are due), their rightful resting-place is the Old Church, in which they were placed by those who bore the brunt and ran the risks of the stirring times which gave them birth.

      Yours obediently
      GEO. BROUGHTON GEE.
Macclesfield,
 October 16th 1912.

****

(Undated letter from an unknown correspondent)

For many years these flags were hung up in the Old Church, until they became very much worn and dilapidated, and at the time of the Church Restoration in 1883 they were removed and handed over to the Hulley family for preservation. Mr. Hulley was Captain Commandant of the Loyal Macclesfield Foresters, who were locally known as "Captain Hulley's Volunteers," from the fact that the regiment was raised and embodied mainly through the devoted energy and loyal patriotism of Jasper Hulley. Esq., of the One House, Buxton Road. Through his zeal and at his cost they became an efficient body of volunteers, animated with a spirit and devotion worthy of that critical period in our country's history. Serving under Commandant Hulley were Major Rowbotham and Captain Boden. The King's Colour was of dark blue silk with the Royal Arms in the centre, and the Regimental Colour was of crimson silk with the Union Jack in the left-hand top corner; in the centre was a wreath of oak leaves and acorns, and the arms of the borough, and underneath the Macclesfield motto, "Nec virtus, nec copia desunt."

Appendix 7 General Report on the Hulley Pedigree
by J. P. Earwaker
Holland Hulley Esq.

Dear Sir
    The papers, which are here copied to illustrate and prove your pedigree, are careful abstracts or copies of the deeds &c. in your possession, with translations of all such as are in Latin, which is the case with nearly all the earlier ones. The numbers in red ink refer to the numbers which I have put in the original deeds. The papers not numbered are extracts of wills &c. preserved at Chester and the whole of the papers are arranged in chronological order, so that any date mentioned in the pedigree will be found in the paper corresponding to that year.

    The earliest deed 1488 is simply a grant of land in Rainow to John Hulley, but in 1490 there is the interesting lease to him of lands &c. then called "one house". This is in English and has been copied in full. The deed next in date c1500 is also in English and is a very curious document of the nature of a will. It is badly written and still more badly spelt but it is very quaint and contains many names relating to the family. There is no trace whatever of the father of John Hulley, but it is quite possible that the family may have been settled in the neighbourhood even earlier than 1844, but no deeds earlier than that have been preserved.

    The subsequent descents probably require little or no comment but it is very noteworthy that those for the first 200 years are almost entirely proved by the deeds so fortunately preserved and had it not been for them it would have been impossible to have traced the pedigree nearly so far back unless the old Rolls of the Halmote Court of Macclesfield had been examined, which would have involved a great amount of labour and expense.

    The number of families, which bore the name of Hulley, Hooley, and Howley, living in or near Macclesfield and who were all probably descended from a common ancestor, is shown by the great number of entries in the Macclesfield Registers. In several instances, two persons bearing the same name, are found living at the same time, which is apt to cause great confusion.

    It is curious to note how certain names have so to speak become hereditary in the family, such as Jasper (derived from the marriage of Katherine daughter of Jasper Willott in 1624 with John Hulley) and Rebecca from the marriage of the first Jasper Hulley with Rebecca Booth in 1661.

    Throughout the pedigree, the main line, that residing at the One House, you will see that I have written Hulley, whilst the younger sons who branched off, are shown bearing the name of Hooley according to the pronunciation and spelling of the period, and which variation they afterwards retained. Your family on the other hand appear to have reverted back to the earlier spelling Hulley sometime in the last century. During the 16th, 17th & 18th centuries the name as will be seen was indifferently spelt Hooley or Howley, but rarely if ever Hulley, as spelt in 1490.

    The family of Jasper Hulley and Macclesfield and Rainow, (the third son of the first Jasper Hulley of the One House) caused me much trouble at the first as many deeds relating to them were preserved with yours, and the trouble was increased by the fact that Jasper Hulley of the One House, the second of that name, married his first cousin, Mary, daughter of Jasper Hooley of Macclesfield. It was the family who supplied the Mayors of Macclesfield named in "East Cheshire" and which presented the font, &c. to the Old Church. It is doubtful whether Jasper Hooley (the son of the elder Jasper Hooley of Macclesfield) had issue, but if not, then this branch of the family is extinct and is now represented by the Newbolds and others as shown in the pedigree.

    I cannot at present trace any connection between the Hooley family of Woodthorpe, co. Notts, or the family of Archbishop Hooley and the Macclesfield families of those names, but it must be borne in mind, as shown by the list of wills now at Chester &c. that families of those names were living at Dukinfield in Cheshire, and also at Adlington, near Macclesfield from early in the 17th century. Neither of these families appear to have attained any position.

                     J. P. Earwaker   Oct 24 81

Appendix 8 Petition for a Grant of Arms 1881

The Memorial of Holland Hulley of The One House
in the Parish of Prestbury, in the County
Palatine of Chester, Gentleman, eldest
son of Jasper Hulley, late of the same
place, Gentleman, deceased

Sheweth

That your Memorialist being desirous of
having Armorial Ensigns duly recorded in the College
of Arms, he therefore requests the favour of Your Grace's
Warrant to the Kings of Arms and Crest as may be proper
to be borne by him and his descendants and by the
other descendants of his father, the said Jasper Hulley
deceased, with due and proper differences according
to the Laws of Arms.

And Your Graces Memorialist shall &c.

(Signed)   Holland Hulley

Grant of Arms 1881

To all and singular to whom these Presents shall
come, Sir Albert William Woods Knight, Garter Principal
King of Arms and Walker Aston Blount Esquire Norroy
King of Arms of the North Parts of England from the River
Trent Northwards Send Greeting Whereas Holland
Hulley of The One House Rainow, Macclesfield in the
Parish of Prestbury in the County Palatine of Chester Gentleman,
eldest son of Jasper Hulley late of the same place Gentleman deceased
hath represented unto the
Most Noble Henry Duke of Norfolk, Earl Marshal
and Hereditary Marshal of England that being desirous
of having Armorial Ensigns duly recorded In the College of
Arms, he therefore requested the favour of His Grace's Warrant
for Our granting and assigning such Arms and Crest
as may be proper to be borne by him and his descendants
and by the other descendants of his father the said
Jasper Hulley deceased according to the Laws of Arms And
forasmuch as the said Earl Marshal did by warrant
under his hand and seal, bearing date the Thirtieth day
of November Last, authorise and direct Us to grant and
assign such Armorial Ensigns accordingly Know ye
therefore that we the said Garter and Norroy in
pursuance of His Grace's Warrant and by virtue of
the Letters Patent of our several Officers to each of Us
respectively granted do by these Presents grant and assign
unto the said Holland Hulley the Arms following
that is to say Sable three Piles Or two issuant from
the Chief and one from the Base each charged

with a Hillock Vert And for the Crest on a wreath of the
Colours A demi-a-mountain reguardant Argent
holding between the pairs an Escocheon Or charged
with a Hillock Vert, as the same are in the margin hereof
more plainly depicted, to be used for ever
hereafter by him the said Holland Hulley and his
descendants and by the other descendants of his father
the said Jasper Hulley deceased, with due and proper
differences according to the Laws of Arms.

In Witness whereof We the said Garter and Norroy
Kings of Arms have to these Presents subscribed Our
names and affixed the Seals of Our several Our
names and affixed the Seals of Our several offices this
Thirteenth day of December in the Forty Fifth year of the
Reign of Our Sovereign Lady Victoria by the Grace of God
of the United Kingdom of Great Britain and Ireland Queen, Defender of the Faith &c. and in
the year of Our Lord
One thousand eight hundred and eighty one.

(Signed) Albert W. Woods Garter   Walter Aston Blount Norroy

Seal   Seal

Endorsed: Recorded in College of Arms London
H. Murray Lane
Chester Herald
Registrar

Appendix 9 Hulley Coat of Arms - Details of Quarterings

(reading from the top, left to right)

First Row
1. HULLEY
2. ARDERNE[1]
3. GLANVILLE (a Glanville was the Justice of all England in the time of Henry SACKVILLE (once Dukes of Dorset, now Earls of Delawarr and Barons Sackville).
4. OREBY (the Justiciar of Chester married the only daughter of Roger, Baron of Montall).
5. MONTALL (he married the heiress of William d'Aubigny, 1st Earl of Lincoln and 1st Earl of Arundel (c. 1109 – 25 September 1176), also known as William d'Albini, who was son of William d'Aubigny, 'Pincerna' (Master Butler of the Royal household) of Old Buckenham Castle in Norfolk, and Maud Bigod, daughter of Roger Bigod, 1st Earl of Norfolk).
6. D'ALBINI
7. ST. HILARY

Second Row
8. HUGH de KEVELIOC, 5th Earl of Chester 1153-1181
9. RANULF de GERNON, 4th Earl of Chester 1129-1153 (–c.1153)
10. RANULF le MESCHIN, 3rd Earl of Chester 1120-1129 (–c.1129)
11. RICHARD d'AVRANCHES, 2nd Earl of Chester 1101-1120 (1094–1120)
12. HUGH d'AVRANCHES, 1st Palatine Earl of Chester 1071-1101 (–1101) also known as le Gros (the fat) and Lupus (Wolf). He was nephew of William the Conqueror. In Normandy he was Earl of d'Avranches.
13. ALFGAR (Earl of Mercia and Cornwall) whose daughter Lucia married Ranulf le Meschin, 3rd Earl of Chester – her aunt married Hugh Lupus, Earl of d'Avranches from which marriage sprung ultimately from Kyvelioc the 5th Earl, by four co-heiresses John Balliol and Robert Bruce, Kings of Scotland, William d'Aubigny Earl of Arundel, Robert de Ferrers Earl of Derby, and William d'Aubigny, 1st Earl of Lincoln – see above. This Lucy, the daughter of Alfgar, was the granddaughter of the great Saxon Leofric, Earl of Mercia, descended from the daughter of Alfred the Great. She was renowned for her beauty and piety – the Lady Godiva.
These latter quarterings came through the marriage of the only child of Oreby, (No. 4.) to Sir Walklin Arderne who held the crest fee of Aldford, Cheshire.
14. KINGSLEY
15. WETTENHALL

Third Row
16. LEIGH of Baguley
17. VENABLES younger son of the Baron of Kinderton
18. LEIGH of Westhall
19. De LEGA
20. SWINEHEAD
21. BAGULEY
22. De CORONA

---

[1] These came from the marriage of Eleanor the daughter of Sir John Donne from whom we had through Mary Arderne the Tarporley property. The Weaver child was a great heiress and a Kings ward – she was given by the King to the first Lord Stanley to marry her as he liked. He chose his 2nd son; her descendants are the Lords of Stanley of Alderley who held the Weaver estates of which Alderley was a portion. Her 2nd husband was Sir John Done (Donne) so the Stanleys and Dones of that day were half-brothers.

23. DONNE (of Utkinton, Tarporley and Flaxyards)[2]

Fourth Row
24. KINGSLEY[3]
25. SYLVESTER (Lord of Stourton and Forester of Wirral).
26. THORNTON
27. KINGSLEY
28. SYLVESTER
29. HELSBY
30. HATTON[4] from whom Sir Christopher and the present Earl of Winchilsea
31. FITZ IVOR

Fifth Row
32. CRISPIN (A great Norman family before the Conquest).
33. LEIGH of Westhall
34. De LEGA
35. ALPERAM (all Donne quarterings but the last – heiress of Mathew Alperham married Thomas Bulkeley of Stanlow. Had one child married to Sir Thomas Arderne of Aldford.
36. DONNE (quarterings the 2nd time until 47th which is Weaver)
37. KINGSLEY
38. SYLVESTER
39. THORNTON

Sixth Row
40. KINGSLEY
41. SYLVESTER
42. HELLESBY
43. HATTON
44. FITZ IVOR
45. CRISPIN
46. WEAVER
47. HULLEY

---

[2] The Dones (twice over) represented the elder branch and came into possession of the Forester's Horn shown on the shield. They were hereditary foresters over Delamere. The Horn was used the last time by a Sir John Done when James I (1603-1625) hunted at Delamere.
[3] From a younger branch of the family of Kingsley the late Charles Kingsley the rector of Eversley claimed descent
[4] The Hattons are descendants of Rolls, Duke of Normandy through Ochrd? (a son of the Earl of Eu) a nephew of the Conqueror and companion in the Conquest.

Appendix 10 The One House Family Tree 1490 to 1927

This Family Tree lists the 107 family members who lived between 1490, when John Hulley first occupied the One House, and 1927 when Arderne, his twelfth generation descendant who had previously emigrated to South Africa, returned to England and died at Southsea, Hampshire.

The tree is too large to be displayed on one page; it is shown on 7 landscape pages thus:

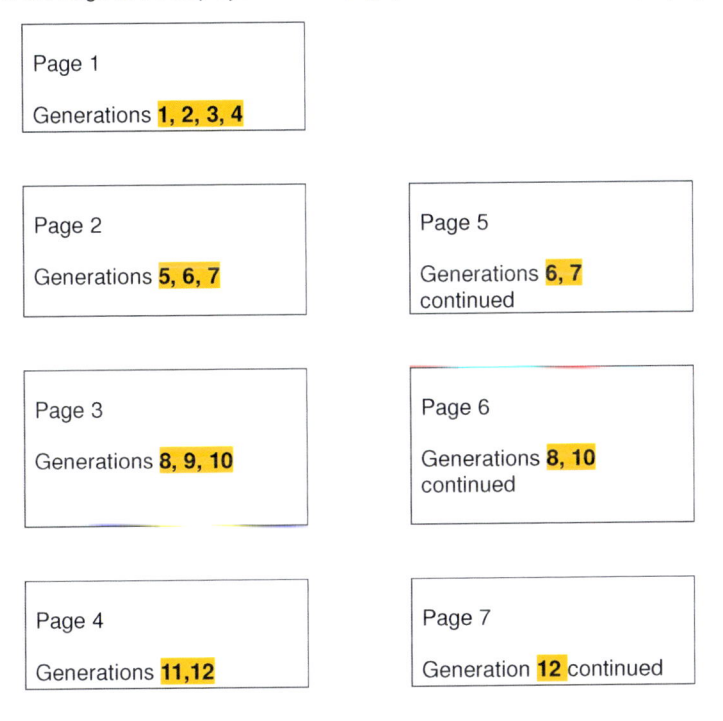

Page 1 Generations 1, 2, 3, 4	
Page 2 Generations 5, 6, 7	Page 5 Generations 6, 7 continued
Page 3 Generations 8, 9, 10	Page 6 Generations 8, 10 continued
Page 4 Generations 11, 12	Page 7 Generation 12 continued

Each person shown on the Family Tree has a set of Notes covering all information discovered about that person. Sources include the following:

The National Archives document classes B – bankrupty; CHES – Cheshire; CRES – Crown Estates; E – Exchequer; HO – Home Office; IR –Inland Revenue; SC – Special Collections; Cheshire Record Office and Archives; John Ryland's Library
Other sources include Electoral registers; Local newspapers; Trades and Commercial Directories; Monumental inscriptions; Parish registers; Family papers; Rate books.

The Notes fill 165 A4 pages, too many to be included in this book, so they are available on my website www.hulley.info. Click on the Family Trees tab on the Home Page and choose Cheshire - Ches01 John Hulley, to open the One House Family Tree. The Notes of each person may be accessed by clicking on their name.

THE ONE HOUSE FAMILY TREE 1490 - 1927

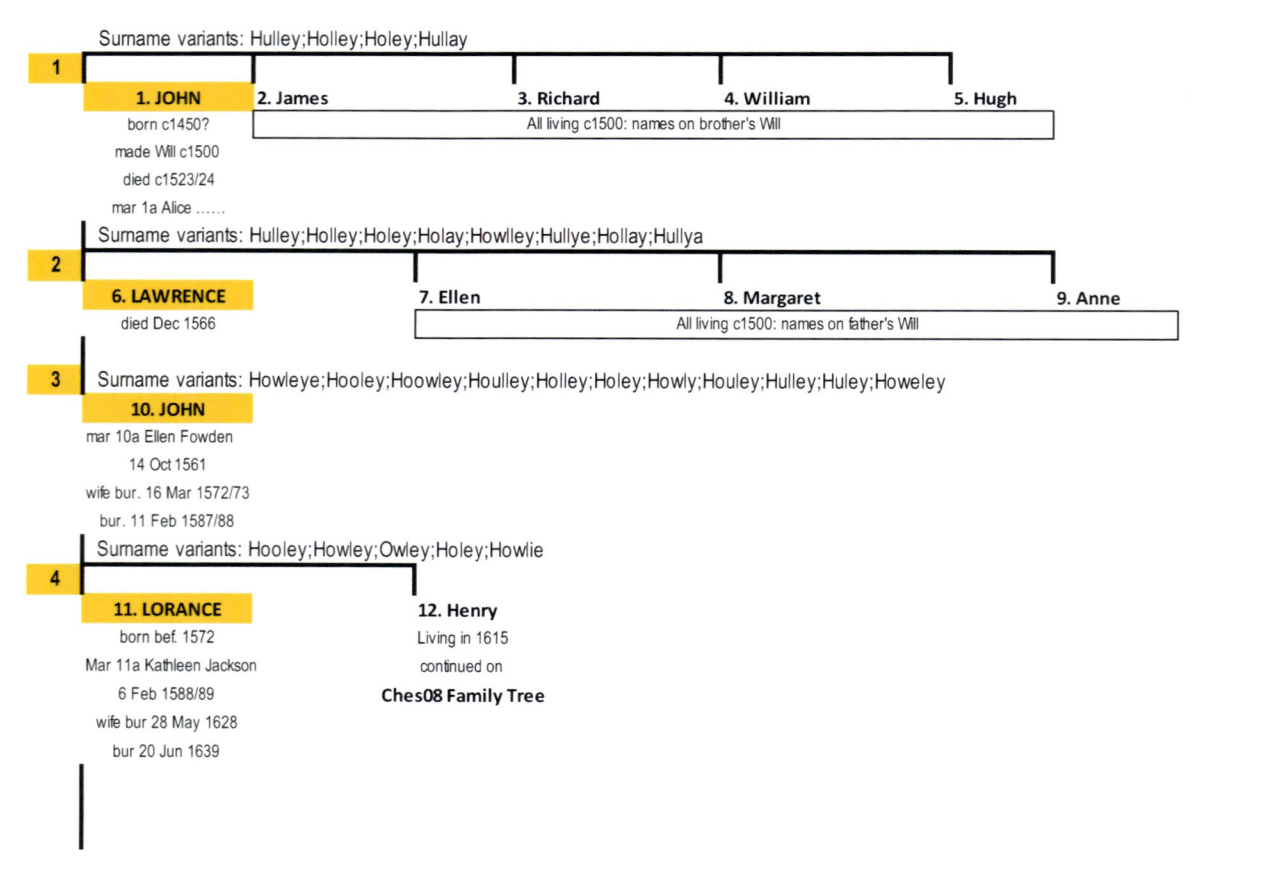

Surname variants: Hulley;Holley;Holey;Hullay

1 **1. JOHN**
born c1450?
made Will c1500
died c1523/24
mar 1a Alice ……..

2. James

3. Richard

4. William
All living c1500: names on brother's Will

5. Hugh

Surname variants: Hulley;Holley;Holay;Howlley;Hullye;Hollay;Hullya

2 **6. LAWRENCE**
died Dec 1566

7. Ellen

8. Margaret
All living c1500: names on father's Will

9. Anne

Surname variants: Howleye;Hooley;Hoowley;Hoouley;Holley;Holey;Howly;Houley;Hulley;Huley;Howeley

3 **10. JOHN**
mar 10a Ellen Fowden
14 Oct 1561
wife bur. 16 Mar 1572/73
bur. 11 Feb 1587/88

Surname variants: Hooley;Howley;Owey;Holey;Howlie

4 **11. LORANCE**
born bef 1572
Mar 11a Kathleen Jackson
6 Feb 1588/89
wife bur 28 May 1628
bur 20 Jun 1639

12. Henry
Living in 1615
continued on
Ches08 Family Tree

Surname variants: Hooley;Howley;Hawley

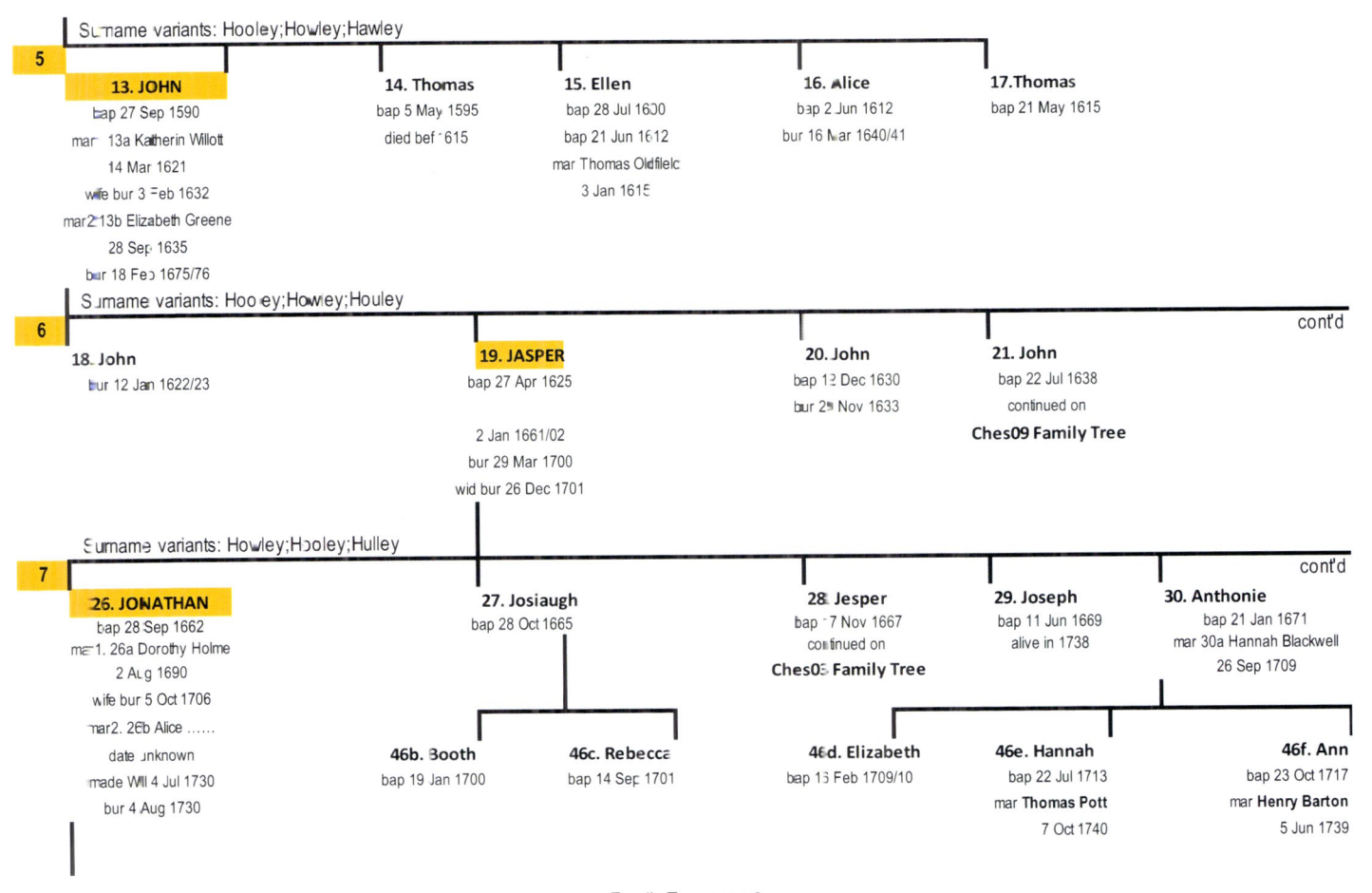

5 | **13. JOHN**
bap 27 Sep 1590
mar 13a Katherin Willott
14 Mar 1621
wife bur 3 Feb 1632
mar2 13b Elizabeth Greene
28 Sep 1635
bur 18 Feb 1675/76

14. Thomas
bap 5 May 1595
died bef 1615

15. Ellen
bap 28 Jul 1630
bap 21 Jun 1612
mar Thomas Oldfield
3 Jan 1615

16. Alice
bap 2 Jun 1612
bur 16 Mar 1640/41

17. Thomas
bap 21 May 1615

Surname variants: Hooley;Howey;Houley

6 | **18. John**
bur 12 Jan 1622/23

19. JASPER
bap 27 Apr 1625

2 Jan 1661/02
bur 29 Mar 1700
wid bur 26 Dec 1701

20. John
bap 12 Dec 1630
bur 2th Nov 1633

21. John
bap 22 Jul 1638
continued on
Ches09 Family Tree

cont'd

Surname variants: Howley;Hooley;Hulley

7 | **26. JONATHAN**
bap 28 Sep 1662
mar1. 26a Dorothy Holme
2 Aug 1690
wife bur 5 Oct 1706
mar2. 26b Alice ……..
date unknown
made Will 4 Jul 1730
bur 4 Aug 1730

27. Josiaugh
bap 28 Oct 1665

46b. Booth
bap 19 Jan 1700

46c. Rebecca
bap 14 Sep 1701

28. Jesper
bap 7 Nov 1667
continued on
Ches05 Family Tree

46d. Elizabeth
bap 13 Feb 1709/10

29. Joseph
bap 11 Jun 1669
alive in 1738

46e. Hannah
bap 22 Jul 1713
mar **Thomas Pott**
7 Oct 1740

30. Anthonie
bap 21 Jan 1671
mar 30a Hannah Blackwell
26 Sep 1709

46f. Ann
bap 23 Oct 1717
mar **Henry Barton**
5 Jun 1739

cont'd

Family Tree page 2

Sumame variants: Howley; Hooley; Hulley

8

35. Hannah
bap 9 Jul 1691
mar Thos Clark
c6 Jul 1710

36. John
(no birth or baptism found)
bur 19 Apr 1693

37. James
bap 22 Jan 1694/95
bur 21 Sep 1706

38. JASPER
bap 8 Oct 1896 [1696]
mar1. 38a Mary Hooley
24 Sep 1730
wife died 15 Apr 1746
mar2. 38b Elizabeth Forster
2 Nov 1750 wife died 5 Nov 1747
mar3. 38c Mary Lowndes
15 Feb 1759 died 1 Feb 1772

39. Willot
(no birth or baptism found)
bur 5 Apr 1700

40. John
bap 19 Dec 1700

cont'd

Sumame variant: Hulley

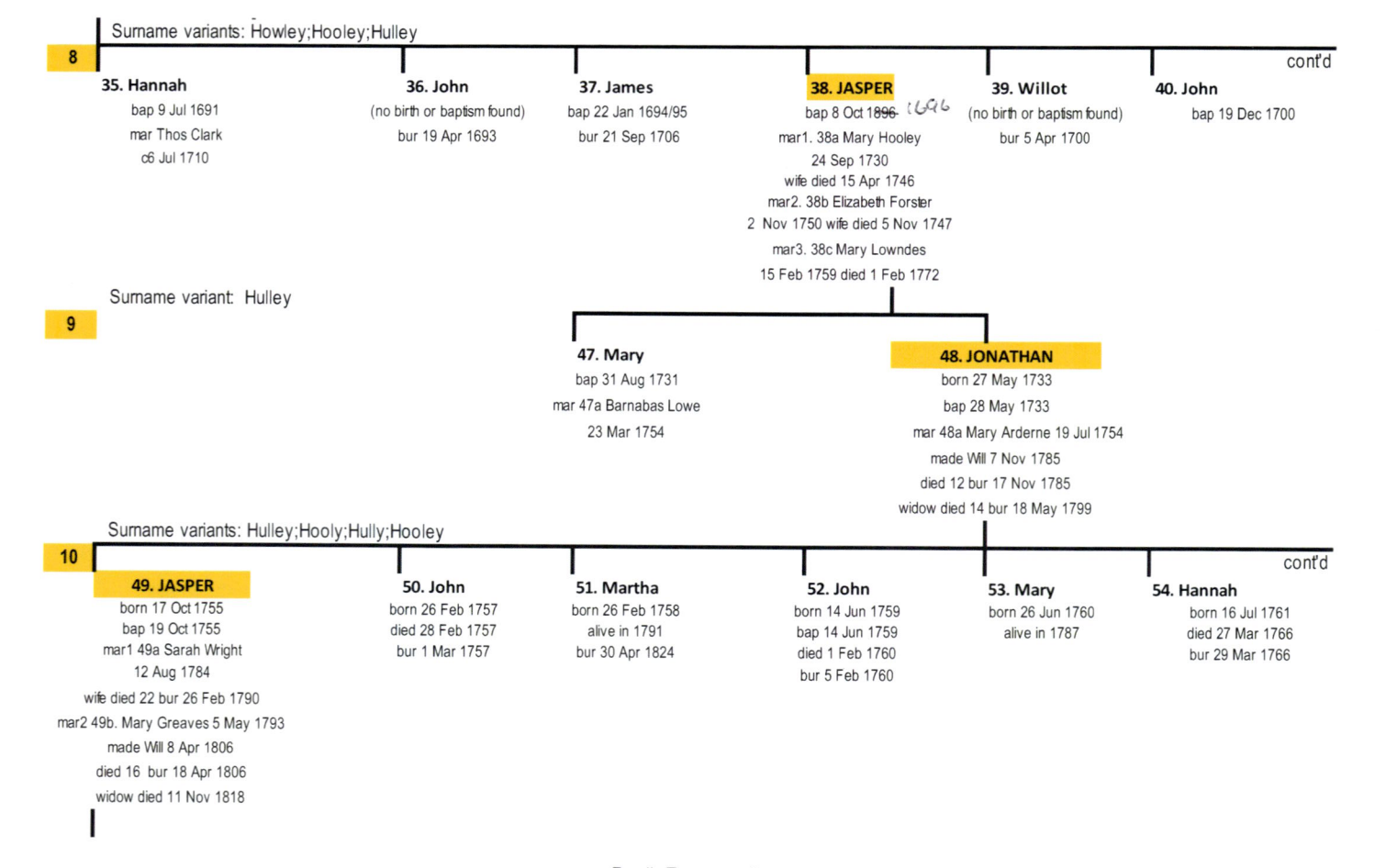

9

47. Mary
bap 31 Aug 1731
mar 47a Barnabas Lowe
23 Mar 1754

48. JONATHAN
born 27 May 1733
bap 28 May 1733
mar 48a Mary Arderne 19 Jul 1754
made Will 7 Nov 1785
died 12 bur 17 Nov 1785
widow died 14 bur 18 May 1799

Sumame variants: Hulley; Hooly; Hully; Hooley

10

49. JASPER
born 17 Oct 1755
bap 19 Oct 1755
mar1 49a Sarah Wright
12 Aug 1784
wife died 22 bur 26 Feb 1790
mar2 49b. Mary Greaves 5 May 1793
made Will 8 Apr 1806
died 16 bur 18 Apr 1806
widow died 11 Nov 1818

50. John
born 26 Feb 1757
died 28 Feb 1757
bur 1 Mar 1757

51. Martha
born 26 Feb 1758
alive in 1791
bur 30 Apr 1824

52. John
born 14 Jun 1759
bap 14 Jun 1759
died 1 Feb 1760
bur 5 Feb 1760

53. Mary
born 26 Jun 1760
alive in 1787

54. Hannah
born 16 Jul 1761
died 27 Mar 1766
bur 29 Mar 1766

cont'd

Family Tree page 3

Surname variant: Hulley

11

58. Jonathan
born 10 Jun 1785
bap 17 Jun 1785
died 21 Dec 1794
bur 26 Dec 1794

59. Jasper
born 2 Dec 1786
bap 2 Dec 1786
died 2 Apr 1793
bur 5 Apr 1793

60. Harriet
born 31 Mar 1788
bap 4 Apr 1788
mar 60a Thomas Whitney
23 Jan 1815
Husband bur 15 Oct 1833
Harriet died 29 Dec 1853
Harriet bur 2 Jan 1854

61. JASPER
born 21 Sep 1794
bap 26 Oct 1794
mar1 61a Ellen Bostock
4 Jul 1821
wife died 28 Dec 1831
wife bur 4 Jan 1832
mar2 61b Maria Holland
30 Nov 1833
made Will 9 Mar 1865
died 11 bur 15 Aug 1867

62. Mary
born 5 Jun 1796
bap 11 Jun 1796
mar 62a Thomas Gorton
5 Jun 1822
Mary died 1 Nov 1846

Surname variant: Hulley

12

63. Ann Goodwin
born 19 Jan 1823
bap 19 Jan 1823
died 21 Jan 1823
bur 23 Jan 1823

64. Jasper
born 24 Mar 1824
bap 15 Apr 1824
died 21 Jan 1849

65. Mary
born 21 Sep 1825
bap 12 Oct 1825
died 27 Feb 1904

66. Ellen Elizabeth
born 7 Feb 1828
bap 12 Mar 1828
died 28 Jan 1837
bur 2 Feb 1837

67. Harriet
born 4 Sep 1831
bap 4 Sep 1831
died 8 Sep 1831
bur 10 Sep 1831

68. Holland
born 16 Sep 1834
bap 15 Oct 1834
died 7 Feb 1904

cont'd

Family Tree page 4

contd. **22. Edward**
bap 25 Feb 1640
mar1 22a Unknown
mar 22b Eliz. Okes
26 Apr 1670
made Will 13 Sep 1684
bur 19 Sep 1684

23. Thomas
bap 13 Jun 1642
continued on
Ches10 Family Tree

24. Charles
(no birth or baptism found)
mar 24a Hester Oldham
15 Jul 1681
made Will 30 Apr 1689
bur 18 May 1689

25. Elizabeth
bur 26 Jun 1665

contd. **31. Samuell**
bap 6 Mar 1673
mar 31a Sarah Heapes mar **Matthew Wheelton**
25 Jul 1692   8 Nov 1715

32. Catherine
bap 19 Apr 1673

33. James
bap Jan 1679/80
continued on
Ches04 Family Tree

34. Abigaell
(no birth or baptism found)
bur 12 Feb 1685/86

34a Elizabeth
bap 10 Dec 1682
mar **Robert Kirkes**
6 Aug 1697

46g Elizabeth
bap 30 Oct 1693

46h Joannis
bur 22 May 1699

46i Samuel
bap 29 Jul 1701
bur 27 Sep 1728

46j Esther
bap 22 Nov 1705
mar **Thos Shrigley**
21 Feb 1731/2

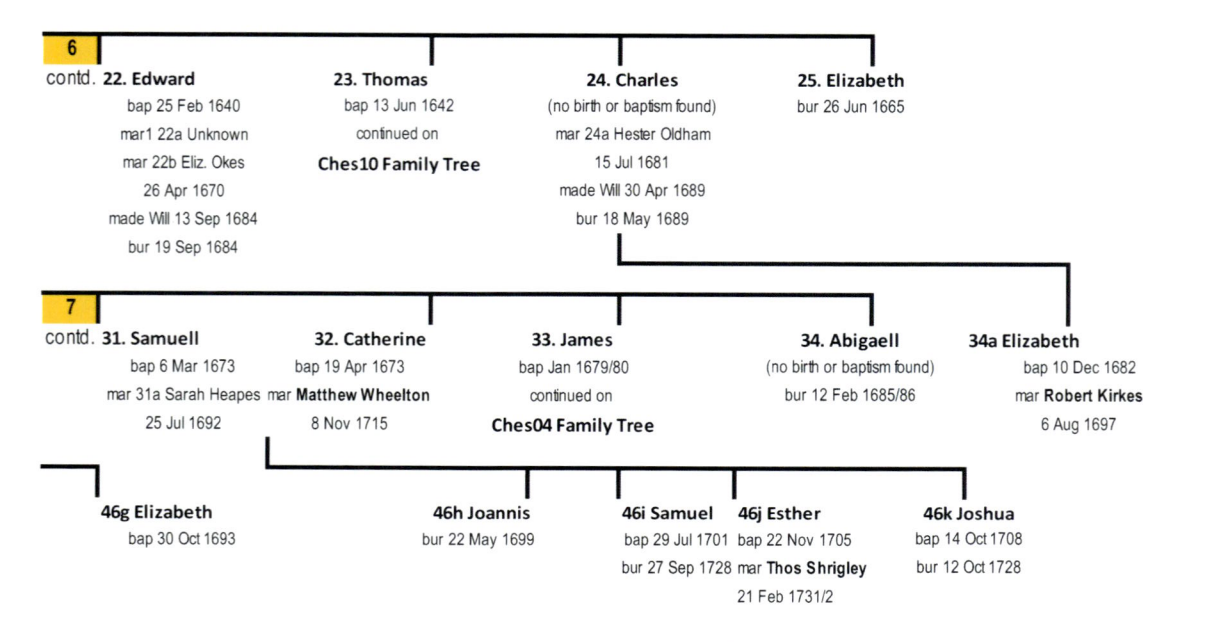

46k Joshua
bap 14 Oct 1708
bur 12 Oct 1728

Family Tree page 5

contd. **41. Mary**
19 Jul 1704
bur 29 May 1726

42. Rebecca
bur 30 Mar 1709

43. Elizabeth
(no birth or baptism found)
mar **Francis Worthington**
2 Mar 1729/30

44. Ameye
bap 5 Mar 1708/09
mar **John Bresne**
13 Oct 1726

45. James
bap 21 Nov 1710
continued on
Ches07 Family Tree

46. Jonathan
bap 1 Aug 1712
mar 46a Mary Littler
7 Jan 1742
bur 6 May 1745

contd. **55. Jonathan**
born 11 Nov 1762
alive in 1785
*moved to Stoke, Staffs

56. Thomas
born 9 Feb 1764
mar 56a Mary Wright
11 Aug 1792
moved to London contd on
London03 Family Tree

57. James
born 15 Feb 1767
bap 17 Feb 1767
died 28 Feb 1767

Family Tree page 6

12 contd.

69. Gorton
born 23 Aug 1835
bap 23 Sep 1835
died 10 May 1836
bur 13 May 1836

70. ARDERNE
born 23 Sep 1836
bap 3 Nov 1836
emigrated to South Africa
(date unknown)
died 20 Feb 1927
crem 24 Feb 1927
continued on
South Africa02 Family Tree

71. Ellen
born 17 Sep 1837
bap 12 Oct 1837
mar1 71a Henry Critchley Broderick
8 Aug 1860
husband died May 1869
mar2 71b John Durham Hall
28 Jul 1874
husband died
she died Mar qtr 1916

72. Maria
born 30 Jun 1839
bap 15 Aug 1839
mar 72a William Chinner
12 Dec 1866
husband died 1906
died Mar qtr 1920

73. Elizabeth
born 30 Sep 1840
bap 17 Nov 1840
mar 73a Rev Fredk Binley Dickinson
16 Jun 1869
died 7 Jul 1879

74. Sarah Anne
born 10 Jul 1843
bap 10 Jul 1843
mar 74a Rev Arthur A. Meurant
24 Aug 1880
she died Dec qtr 1909

Family Tree page 7

Index

1611 Survey of the Manor and Forest of Macclesfield, 1, 2, 9
Adlington, 4, 45, 62
Alford, Mr., 20
Anhus, 2
Ann, 29
Arderne, 25
Arderne, John, 16
Arderne, Mary, 16
Arnold, Widow of Peter, 24
Ashton under Lyne, 45
Awterspoole, 1
Barber, Mr., 14
Barfield Leys, 24
Barnes, Thomas, 24
barr field, the, 56
Barrfield, the, 10, 12
Barrfield, the meadow, 12
Benedict and Roger de Onhus, 2
Bennett, Benjamin, 19
Bennett, Joseph, 26
Dillinge, 11
Blackley, 12
Blount, Walter Aston, 64
Boden, Captain, 61
Bohun, Humphrey de, 2
Bollington, 8, 58
Bombay Army, 29
Bombay Staff Corps, 30
Booth, Rebeccah, 11, 12, 62
Booth, William, 14, 38
Boothby, Peter, 19
Boothby, Robert, 19
Boothby, William, 11
Bosden Brook, 1
Boslegh, 4
Bosley, 4
Bostock, Ellen, 25
Bott Field, 24
Bottfield deeds, 34
Bottfield House Farm, 26
Bottfield meadow, the, 13
Braddock, Thomas, 13
Bredbury, 4
Bresne, John, 16
Brocon, Wyllyam de Brynow, 6
Brink, The, 19
Broadhead, James, 26
Brocklehurst, 36
Broderick, Henry Critchley, 29
Bromley Davenport, vi, 4
Brontnall, Judith, 10
Brookes, Mr. G., 42
Burgess of Macclesfield, 16
Burgess, Elizabeth, 8
Butley, 2, 4
Buxton Road, v, 16, 46, 60, 61
Buxton, Miss Ethel, 36, 38
Calveley, 8, 9, 56, 57
Castleton, Derbyshire, 6

Cheshire Archives and Local Studies, ii, 4, 31
Cheshire Electoral Registers, 25
Cheshire Rifle Volunteers, 21
Chester, vii, 4, 8, 9, 14, 20, 25, 32, 37, 62, 63
Chester Herald, 64
Chinner, Mrs, 35
Chinner, The late Mr Howard, 30
Chinner, William, 29, 34
Christ Church, Macclesfield, 30
Clark, Thomas, 16
Cliff Road, the, 12
Clowes, William, 10
Coal mines, 26
Coat of Arms, v, 31, 34, 65, 67
College of Arms, 31, 32, 64
Consistory Court at Chester, 20
Court Leet, 13, 16
Coventry Priory, 2
CRO, vi, vii, 6, 9, 10, 11, 13, 15, 16, 20
Cromwell Wood, 1
Crumwell, 1
Cunningham, Mr., 45
Dane, 1, 3
Davemport, Arthur, 57
Davemport, Rafe, 57
Davenport Deeds, 2, 48, 49, 50, 51, 52, 53
Davenport family, 2
Davenport, Arthur, 9
Davenport, Hugh, 1, 2, 4, 8, 56
Davenport, John de, 2
Davenport, Margery, 2
Davenport, Ralph, 4
Davenport, Richard, 1
Davenport, Richard de, 1
Davenporte, Arthur, 10
Davernport, Hugh, 57
Davernport, Rauf, 56
Davernporte, Arthur, 56
Davernporte, Margere, 56
Deane, Peter, 12
Derby, 6, 30, 34, 65
Dickinson, Revd. Frederick Bonley, 29
Disley Stanley, 58
Dispute in 1755-57, 20
Dokinfeld, 4, 45
Downes, John, 20
Dublin Gazette, 21
Duke of Norfolk, Henry, 63
Dukinfield, 4, 45, 62
Duncalf Thomas, 2
Dundas Henry, 22
Earl Hugh, 2
Earl of Chester, 1, 65
Earl of Derby, 58
Earl of Stamford and Warrington, 22
Earles, John, 60
Earls of Chester, 1
Earwaker, John, 8, 11, 20, 31, 48, 49, 50, 51, 52, 53, 58, 62
Eddesbury, 24

Eddesbury Lane Farm, 24
Eddisbury Hall, 16, 33
Eddisbury Lane Farm, 26
Edesburie Grounds, 10
Edesbury, 13
Edsbury Lane, 16
Fauconberg, Lady Bridget Viscountess Dowager, 13, 14, 15, 16, 38
Feast of St Michael, 2
Fitton Edward, 2
Fitton Hugh, 2
Fitton Margaret, 2
Forster, Elizabeth, 16
Fowden, Ellen, 7
Foxwist, 4
Frostcroft the, 12
Gawsworth, 1, 11
Gee, Geo. Broughton, 61
General Report on the Hulley Pedigree, 31, 62
Gibbon, Matthew, 26
Gibbons, Annie Margarite, 34
Gibbons, Constance, 34
Girdshawe Brooke, 10
Goodshaw, 12
Goodshaw messuage, The, 19
Gorton, 25
Goyt, 1, 3
Great Edsbury, 12
Great Haybay, 12
Great Moore, 12
Greaves, Robert, 24
Greene, Elizabeth, 10
Griffith, Elizabeth, 10
Griffith, William, 10
Grove Farm, 2, 19, 24, 26
Guernsey, iv, 25, 27, 28
Guhuz (One House) Gilbert de, 2
Hale, 4
Hall, Lieut. Col. J. Durham, 30, 34
Hall, Mrs E. Durham, 35
Hammersley, Martha, 24
Har Edsbury, 16, 19
Heald, William, 24
Heaton-Smith, Richard, 33
Hesford, Thomas, 24
Hewley, Sir John, 31
Heywood, Hannah, 15
Higginbottom, Henry, 20
High Constable of Macclesfield Hundred, 25
High Low Farm, 1
High Peak, 1
Higher House Barn, 12
Higher Moor, 34
Hodgson, Bryan, 16
Holey, Ad de, 3
Holey, Robus de, 3
Holeye, 3
Holeye, John de, 3
Holeye, Matilda de, wife of John, 2, 3
Holeye, William de, 2, 3, 65
Holeye/Holey, William de, 3
Holland, Jasper Loton, 25
Holland, Loton, 28
Holland, Maria, 25
Holland, Philip, 25, 28
Hollay, Ad de, 3
Hollay, Adam de, 3
Holme, Dorothy, 11
Holme, James, 11
Holy, Roba del, 3
Hooley Hill, 45
Hooley, Amye, 16
Hooley, Dorothy, 13
Hooley, Elizabeth, 16
Hooley, Hannah, 16
Hooley, James, 16, 45
Hooley, Jasper, 13, 15, 16, 62
Hooley, John, 10, 15, 16, 45
Hooley, Jonathan, 13, 15, 16
Hooley, Laurance, 9
Hooley, Lawrence, 9
Hooley, Lawrentius, 10
Hooley, Maria, 16
Hooley, Rebecca., 13
Hooley, Samuel, 16
Hooley, Susanna, 16
Hooley, Thomas, 15, 16
Hooley/Howley, Henry, 7, 8
Hooley/Howley, John, 3, 4, 7, 8, 9, 45
Hooley/Howley, Lawrence, 7, 8
Hooley/Hulley, Alexander, 24
Hooley/Hulley, Jasper, 24
Hordern, 10, 25
Houley, John, 10
Howeley, Elizabeth, 15
Howley, Abigail, 11
Howley, Alice, 15
Howley, Alicia, 9
Howley, Anthony, 11
Howley, Booth, vii, 12
Howley, Charles, 11
Howley, Edward, 10, 11
Howley, Elizabeth, 10, 15
Howley, Ellen, 9
Howley, Hannah, 15
Howley, James, 11, 45
Howley, Jasper, 9, 10, 11, 12, 15, 45
Howley, Jasper junior, 11
Howley, Johes, 7
Howley, John, 9, 10, 11
Howley, Jonathan, 11, 12, 15
Howley, Joseph, 11
Howley, Josiah, 11, 12
Howley, Josuah, 15
Howley, Katherine, 10
Howley, Kathleen, 9
Howley, Laurance, 8
Howley, Laurence, 7
Howley, Lawrence, 9, 10
Howley, Mary, 15
Howley, Miles, 45
Howley, Rebecca, 12
Howley, Rebeccah, 15
Howley, Samuel, 11
Howley, Sara, 15
Howley, Thomas, 11, 15
Howley, William, 15, 45
Howley,John, 10, 15
Hule, John, 31
Huley, John, 31

Hull, Adam del, 3
Hulleson, Roba, 3
Hulley, Alice, 6, 16, 57
Hulley, Ann, 6
Hulley, Annes, 57
Hulley, Arderne, 33, 34, 35, 36, 60
Hulley, Captain, 22
Hulley, Done, 28
Hulley, Elizabeth, 25, 29
Hulley, Ellen, 6, 25, 29, 30, 34
Hulley, Ellen Gorton, 34
Hulley, Ellyn, 57
Hulley, Hannah, 16
Hulley, Harriet, 25
Hulley, Holland, v, 11, 25, 28, 29, 30, 31, 32, 34, 48, 49, 50, 51, 52, 53, 62, 63, 64
Hulley, Hugh, 6, 57
Hulley, James, 6, 16, 26, 45, 57
Hulley, Jasper, iv, 13, 14, 15, 16, 19, 20, 21, 22, 23, 24, 25, 27, 28, 29, 31, 33, 38, 61, 62, 63, 64
Hulley, Jasper junior, 24
Hulley, Jasper M., ii, 31, 32
Hulley, John, vii, 2, 3, 4, 6, 10, 16, 56, 57, 62
Hulley, Jonathan, 13, 16, 19, 20, 37, 43
Hulloy, Lawrence, 6, 7, 10, 45, 56, 57
Hulley, Margaret, 6, 57
Hulley, Maria, 16, 25, 27, 28, 29, 30, 34
Hulley, Martha, 16, 20
Hulley, Mary, 16, 20, 25, 27, 29, 30, 34
Hulley, Mary widow, 24
Hulley, Richard, 1, 2, 6, 57
Hulley, Sarah Ann, 25, 27, 30, 33
Hulley, Thomas, 16, 19, 20
Hulley, William, 6, 57
Hulley's Volunteers, 22, 60, 61
Hulme, John, 11
Hurdsfield, 11, 12, 16, 24, 51, 58
Hyde, 4
Ingarsley, 10
Inland Revenue, v, 35, 36
Irvine, W.F., 2
Islington, St Mary's, 14
Jackson, John, 11, 19
Jackson, Kathleen, 8
Jackson, Thomas, 10
Jenkins, Ann, 13, 14
Jenkins, Edward, 13
Jenkinson, Frank, 35
Jersey, 27
John Rylands Library, ii, 4, 22
Johnson, John, 10
Katherine Wheel Inn, Bishopsgate Street, 14
Kerridge, 11, 30
Kettleby, Mr, 14
Kettleshulme, 4, 21, 58, 59
Keyridge, 13
Keyridgend, 13
Kirk, John, 26
Knoll Nook, 26
Knolle House, 2
Knollnook, 10
Knowl Field, 35
Knowl, the further, 12
Knowles, Richard, 33
Kyvelioc, Hugh, 1

Lancashire and Cheshire Record Society, 1
Latus, William, 13
Lawley, Eliza, 14
Lay Subsidy Roll, 45
Leek, 1
Legh, Peter, 20, 21, 59
Legh, Rog., 56
Little Cliffe, the, 12
London, 3, 13, 14, 16, 31, 32, 34, 64
London Chronicle, 21
Lord Derby, 59
Lord Lieutenant of Cheshire, 22
Lowe, John, 10
Lowe, Joseph, 13
lower field, the, 56
Lower Moor, 34
Lowndes, Mary, 16
Loyal Macclesfield Foresters, 60, 61
Loyal Macclesfield Volunteer Infantry, 21, 22, 60
Lunt, Mr, 14
Lyme Hall, 20
Lyme Handley, 58, 59
Macclesfield, 1, iv, v, vi, vii, 1, 2, 3, 4, 6, 8, 9, 10, 11, 12, 15, 16, 20, 21, 22, 23, 26, 31, 33, 35, 36, 45, 47, 49, 50, 51, 52, 53, 58, 59, 60, 61, 62, 63
Macclesfield Common, 20
Macclesfield Corps, 21
Macclesfield Courier, 25, 26, 60
Macclesfield Courier and Herald, 23
Macclesfield Express, ii
Macclesfield Eyre Roll, 3
Macclesfield Forest, 1, 2, 3, 6, 10, 45, 58, 59
Macclesfield Park, 20
Macclesfield Times, 38, 44
Malfilastre, Roger, 2
Marble Font, 15
Marple, the, 13
Marsh Rails, 24
Master Forester, 1
Matilda, Hugh's mother, 2
Meurant, Rev. Arthur A., 30, 34
Meurant, Sarah Ann, 34
Minor, Richard, 30
Moneyash, Derbyshire, 15
Moore, the, 12
Mottershead, Jeffery, 24
Mottram, 4
Mottram Andrew, 4
Mottram, Peter, 45
myddle field, the, 56
National Archives, The, ii, vii, 3, 6, 10, 22
New Bond Street, 14
Newton, 4
Norbury, 4
Norbury, Samuel, 19
North Rode, 3
Oakes, Elizabeth, 10
Oakes, John, 33
Oakes, Sarah, 11
Otferton, 3
Oldfield, James, 10
Oldfield, Thomas, 9
Oldham, Hester, 11
Onhuz, 2

70

Orrey, Rt. Hon. Lord, 14
Passlegh, John de, 2
Pearson, Captain James, 21
Pearson, John, 14
Pennines, 1, 3
Pott Shrigley, 20, 58
Pott, Robert, 20
Poynton, 4
Prestbury, 1, 7, 9, 10, 58, 59, 63
Preston, George, 24
Price, Mr Justice, 16
Prince William Frederick, 22
Rainow, 1, vi, vii, 2, 4, 6, 9, 10, 11, 13, 15, 16, 20, 25, 26, 32, 35, 37, 45, 58, 59, 62, 63
Rainow Poor House, 16
Ranow, 6, 7, 8, 9, 10, 13
Ranowe, vii, 8, 10, 11, 12
Regarder of Macclesfield Forest, 3
Rhodes, Alice, 26
Rhodes, John, 19, 24
Richard the son of Earl Robert of Gloucester, 2
River Dean, 16
River Mersey, 3
Rode, 1
Roe, Charles, 16
Roefield meadow, the, 13, 16
Rowbotham, Major, 61
Rowson, Thomas, 19
Rushey meadow, the, 13, 16
Saltersbridge, 1
Savage, Thomas, 6
Serjeant's Inn, 16
Shady Yard Green (Sutton), 24
Shakespeare, William, 16
Sharpley or Lower Fields, 20
Shaw, Elizabeth, 2
Shaw, Joan, 2
Shaw, William, 2
Sheldon, Joseph, 24
Sheldon, Mrs, 26
Sherratt, Messrs. and Co., 42
Showre, Johem, 6
Shrigley, 4, 58, 59
Smith, Walter, 38
Somerford, 3, 4, 51
Somerford, Thomas de, 3
South Africa, ii, 8, 9, 28, 31, 34, 36
Southsea, 36
Spering family, 36
Sprinck meadow, the, 13
Stafford, John, 16

Staffordshire Moorlands, 1
Stalagh, 4
Stalybridge, 4
Stamford, Lord, 22
Stockport, 3
Stoke upon Trent, 20
Sutton, 10, 13, 14, 16, 24, 36, 58, 59
Sutton Hall, 13, 14
Sutton, Martha, 24
Swanscoe, 13
Swindells, William, 19
Swine Park, 20
Taylor, James, 19
Titherington, 9, 10
Tompson, Edward, 13
Toot Hill, 1
Toothill, the, 12
Tower Hill, 16
Trotter, William, 60
Turner, Thomas, 8
Two Ridge Meadows, 24
Vale Royal, 24
Walker Barn, 24
Walker, Edward, 12
walle field, the, 56
Walln House in Rainow, 13
Warren, Joseph, 19
Warrington, 22
Warwickshire, 16
Watson, Francis, 11
Watson, William, 13
Watson's meadows, 13
Weldon, Willliam de, 2
Whaley, 58
Whaley Bridge, 1
Wild, Robert, 38
Wildboarclough, 1, 58, 59
Wildboreclough, 20
Wilkinson, John, 19
Willott, Jasper, 9, 62
Willott, Katherine, 9
Wilmslow, 11
Wincle, 58
Windyway Head, 19, 24, 26
Winkle, 58, 59
Wolverhampton, 29, 34
Wood, JP, Mr T. W., 36
Woods, Albert W., 64
Woods, William, 63
Worthington, Francis, 16